DATE D

1980

DYNAMICS OF TELEVISION

For Sheila and Sandra

Dynamics of television

JON BAGGALEY
BA, PhD, ABPsS
Centre for Communication Studies
University of Liverpool

STEVE DUCK
MA, PhD, ABPsS
Department of Psychology
University of Lancaster

SAXON HOUSE

Published by
SAXON HOUSE, Teakfield Limited
Westmead, Farnborough, Hants., England.

Reprinted 1978

ISBN 0 566 00124 1
Library of Congress Catalog Card Number 76-20921
Printed in Great Britain by Biddles Ltd., Guildford

Contents

List of tables

List of figures

Preface

The earliest origin of this book may be traced to the University of Sheffield in 1971, when one of the authors trained a hidden TV camera to observe the other at his desk. Despite this deception, we have continued in a joint investigation of television's psychological impact since leaving Sheffield for posts elsewhere in Communication Studies and Social Psychology. As psychologists our respective interests in perceptual and social processes diverge, though in the study of television they are related, and approaches drawn from both fields of enquiry form the basis of this book.

Much has been written about the effects of television since its public inauguration in 1936 — reasonably so, in view of the evidence that television viewing occupies on average more of our time than any other leisure pursuit. As the prime information source for a substantial majority of the population, the medium's central role in society is increasingly apparent; and as the most sophisticated of our modern media, appealing with immediacy to the two most basic senses at once, its ability to intrigue and absorb the individual is beyond question. But analysts of television's effects have gone further, attributing to the medium psychological powers to control our attitudes and actions, and evoking alarming visions of future media dependence. Such prophecies may certainly one day prove accurate: in situations where the individual gains his information from a single source and via a single channel its compulsiveness is strong indeed, since the individual is thereby deprived of any other criteria by which to test its content. Television, therefore, in an environment starved of all other information channels, has as great a capacity for social control as any medium, and, chilling as the image of a society ruled by media can be, it is not surprising that authors have continually emphasised this capacity.

Media research, however, has been strikingly inconclusive. Focused primarily on the three areas of social effect where the media's capacity for control is most feared — namely advertising, electioneering and social violence — studies of the media invariably attract public interest, but have little political impact. The basic problem is the same as with any young science: before its laws can be established, the science needs to define the variables that are the stuff of its study. As in psychology generally, the human processes under examination in media studies still lack a unified theoretical base despite twenty years of intense investigation.

The shortcomings of media research are seen in relief on examination of the thorniest of traditional questions – the relationship between television and social violence. In its 1955 investigation a sub-committee of the US Senate proclaimed that almost a quarter of broadcast television contained violence of one sort or another (Shulman, 1975): yet it is immediately clear that such statistics must depend on definitions of violence that are capable of fluctuating according to the criteria set by each particular individual investigator, or longitudinally according to external social standards. Ten years later, a Senate report indicated that the proportion of programmes containing violence was by then nearly a half: but on this occasion only peak-hour viewing was analysed, so a strict comparison between this and the earlier finding is impossible on this basis alone. In 1969, the President's Commission on the Causes and Prevention of Violence declared uncompromisingly: 'Violence on television encourages violent forms of behaviour and fosters moral and social values about violence in family life which are unacceptable in a civilised society.' Yet, as acknowledged elsewhere in the commission's report, there is no evidence that television is an actual *cause* of social violence; for, as in the million-dollar Surgeon-General's report that followed in 1972, the commission's findings were purely correlative, equating the two main factors in what is scientifically a pretty arbitrary fashion. As Eysenck and Eysenck (1964) indicate: 'Correlational analyses are important, but they are merely permissive, not compelling', and they invoke Thurstone's maxim that 'a correlation is a confession of ignorance'.

When a subject compels public concern but contains no indisputable facts and combines with a state of ignorance in this way, urgent assumptions can be made and mountainous theory based upon them. Moreover, the more mountainous the intentions behind a theory, the more elastic it becomes. The most substantial theoretical contributions often lead paradoxically to a fallow period within the science when research becomes less questioning, and is channelled in directions laid down by the dominant theory alone. The study of television has suffered dramatically in this fashion. Since the 1950s media research in general has been dominated by the distinctive contribution of Marshall McLuhan. Using the techniques of analogy and juxtaposition perfected by the advertisers of whom he writes, McLuhan pieces together a rich mix of literary, historical and sociological observations from which the (hypothetical) cause and effect of media's role in society is readily inferred. His view of the relationship between man and the media is straightforwardly deterministic. Technology, McLuhan argues, has re-tribalised mankind on a worldwide scale: within the 'global village' to which he now belongs, man's perceptions and aspirations are shaped by the media that bind the tribe together. The effects of the media are thus to be observed in the behaviour of the mass; and McLuhan's viewpoint has directed the study of mass communications and the mass media to this day. It is, however, only one viewpoint, and as such should be placed in context.

For there is a tendency in science to start from one particular viewpoint, using particular methodology to tackle but one problem out of the many that exist. Predictably, this means not only that areas of study begin to suffer from 'hardening of the categories' but also that they tend increasingly to ignore the possible benefits they could derive from other academic disciplines characterised by different theoretical approaches, different terminologies and different empirical schemata. The need at present for some kind of infusion into the communications field from other specialist areas of the social sciences is indicated by a dissatisfaction with the progress and style of conventional communication research now becoming apparent. Williams (1973) has indicated that current research approaches skirt the edge of communication problems, failing to allow any effective analysis of 'specific modern communications conventions and forms'. The study of communications, he argues, 'was deeply and almost disastrously deformed' by its connection with the notion 'mass'. Indeed, under the microscope of social psychology, we find, not surprisingly, that group behaviour is a dynamic process of the most complex type: the behaviour of group members is subject to numerous influences and variations, which McLuhan for one seems not to have suspected. In attempts, therefore, to understand the impact of any communication medium in terms of its effects on a large 'mass', many of its more basic and differing effects on the *individual* members of its audience are quite obscured. Clearly, in order to bring our understanding of media processes into line with other areas of communication theory we must first of all view them through the same psychological microscope.

This then is the prime aim of this book: to examine media effects in the dynamic human and social context to which they belong. The book is written at a time when the study of communication is spiced with a feeling of keen anticipation. Developments in the techniques and technology of social science suggest that an appraisal of the media's social psychological impact is now due. We feel that the joining together of our own two specialist areas, and the discussions that led us away from the traditional areas of media research, have given us a new perspective on the dynamics of television which lead to a re-evaluation of what the central issues ought to be. The research on which the book is partly based concerns that very area of media studies which previous emphases on 'the mass' have obscured: an analysis of the effects upon the individual that stem from the conventions and forms of a medium as opposed to its declared content − in particular the ways in which these conventions and forces affect the individual's processes of cognition and social judgement. We concentrate within this framework on the dynamic effects of television specifically, although we suspect that the effects of other media are essentially the same. Though our primary viewpoints are within fields of perceptual and social psychology, the study of communication processes naturally draws upon many other fields of enquiry and it is in the nature of an interdisciplinary science − especially one only recently pressed into being − that there is of course no one audience ready made to receive it. Thus readers with interests and background knowledge in specific areas that we discuss may choose to consider the implications of certain sections of the book in more detail than others. Nonetheless, it is to be hoped that some of the excitement of work between disciplines is conveyed in the pages generally.

In planning the book we have been grateful that two of the most daunting tasks in this area have now been spared us. The first, a detailed discussion of the problems and pitfalls of media research to date, has been most effectively accomplished by Howitt and Cumberbatch (1975); via a specific focus on the relationship between media and violence touched on above, they uncover many of the assumptions and methodological inadequacies of media research in general, and raise questions of its political value far beyond their point of departure. The second problem, that of extracting some sense from the endless audience research figures that the major broadcasting organisations produce, has been tackled by Goodhardt, Ehrenberg and Collins (1975). Their inspection of audience data collected between 1967 and 1975 for the Independent Broadcasting Authority reveals patterns of viewing previously unsuspected and refutes several notions about television's effects that have been traditionally assumed. Their work provides an objective statistical basis for the examination of television's dynamic properties henceforward. A third writer whose recent contributions to the field we would like to acknowledge is Raymond Williams. His analyses of media content − notably in *Communications* (1966) and *Television* (1974) − provide a valuable base for our study of the TV message in chapter 2. Williams' discussions, in the latter work particularly, of some of the medium's 'intrinsic visual experiences, for which no conventions and no mode of description have been prepared or offered' lay down a gauntlet which the present book attempts to grasp.

These then are our literary debts. At the personal level we wish particularly to acknowledge the help of our colleagues, notably Dr Harry Jamieson and Mr John Thompson of Liverpool University: their advice and encouragement have influenced the book in numerous valuable ways. We would also like to thank Dr Neil Johnson of Lancaster University who, despite several publishing commitments of his own, was always willing to listen and give valuable advice; and Ken Duck who offered his expertise generously and generated many fruitful discussions through his incisive observation. Throughout the final stages of the work we have leaned heavily on the support of Miss Margaret Cran whom we would like to thank most sincerely for her work on the schedule and personal construct analyses, and on the bibliography; likewise Mrs Margaret Johnson for her most generous assistance with the preparation of the manuscript in all its versions. We gratefully acknowledge Mrs Jill Cox and the technical assistance of both of our Departments for the additional help with the manuscript and in the experimental work we have reported. Our especial gratitude goes to our wives, Sheila and Sandra, and children, for their fortitude and understanding throughout the work and for keeping us in touch with events on television as writing about it replaced viewing it at the centre of our lives. Finally we acknowledge the debt to our parents — who always said we watched too much anyway!

JPB, SWD
June, 1976.

References

Eysenck, H. J. and Eysenck, S. B. G. (1964), *Manual: Eysenck Personality Inventory*, London, University of London Press.

Goodhardt, G. J., Ehrenberg, A. S. C. and Collins, M. A. (1975), *The Television Audience: Patterns of Viewing*, Farnborough, Saxon House.

Howitt, D. and Cumberbatch, G. (1975), *Mass Media Violence and Society*, London, Paul Elek.

National Commission on the Causes and Prevention of Violence (1969), report, US Government Printing Office, Washington DC.

Shulman, M. (1975), *The Ravenous Eye*, London, Coronet.

Surgeon-General's Report (1972), *Television and Social Behavior,* US Government Printing Office, Washington DC.

Williams, R. (1966), *Communications*, London, Pelican.

Williams, R. (1973), 'Cultural studies and communication', paper read to the International Conference on the Future of Communication Studies, Heathrow, London.

Williams, R. (1974), *Television: Technology and Cultural Form*, London, Fontana.

Copyright acknowledgements

Material from the following sources has been reproduced by kind permission of the publishers. (Joint publications by the authors form the substance of chapter 4.)

Baggaley, J. P.:
  (1973a) 'Analysing TV presentation techniques for educational effectiveness', *Educational Broadcasting International*, vol. 6, no. 3 (British Council).
  (1973b) 'Developing an effective educational medium', *Programmed Learning and Educational Technology*, vol. 10 (Association for Programmed Learning and Educational Technology).
  (1975) 'Access to the Looking-glass', *Educational Broadcasting International*, vol. 8, no. 2 (British Council).

Baggaley, J. P. and Duck, S. W.:
  (1974) 'Experiments in ETV: effects of adding background', *Educational Broadcasting International*, vol. 7, no. 4 (British Council).
  (1975a) 'Communication effectiveness in the educational media', in Baggaley, J. P., Jamieson, G. H. and Marchant, H. (eds), *Aspects of Educational Technology*, Pitman (Association for Programmed Learning and Educational Technology).
  (1975b) 'Experiments in ETV: effects of edited cutaways', *Educational Broaasting International*, vol. 8, no. 1 (British Council).
  (1975c) 'Psychological effects of image variations', *Video and Film Communication*, March (Screen Digest Limited).
  (1975d) 'Experiments in ETV: further effects of camera angle', *Educational Broadcasting International*, vol. 8, no. 4 (British Council).

Baggaley, J. P., Jamieson, G. H. and Marchant, H. (eds):
  (1975) *Aspects of Educational Technology VIII*, Pitman, (Association for Programmed Learning and Educational Technology).

Duck, S. W. and Baggaley, J. P.:
  (1974a) 'Persuasive Polish', *New Society*, 18 July (New Science Publications).
  (1974b) 'ETV production methods vs. educational intention', *Educational Broadcasting International*, vol. 7, no. 3 (British Council).

(1975a) 'Audience reaction and its effect on perceived expertise', *Communication Research*, vol. 2, no. 1 (Sage Publications Inc.).
(1975b) 'Experiments in ETV: interviews and edited structure', *Educational Broadcasting International*, vol. 8, no. 2 (British Council).
(1975c) 'Experiments in ETV: effects of camera angle', *Educational Broadcasting International*, vol. 8, no. 3 (British Council).

Jamieson, G. H., Thompson, J. O. and Baggaley, J. P.:
(1976) 'Intention and interpretation in the study of communication', *Journal of Educational Television*, vol. 2, no. 1 (National Educational Closed-Circuit Television Association).

Thompson, J. O., Baggaley, J. P. and Jamieson, G. H.:
(1975) 'Representation, review, and the study of communication', *Journal of Educational Television*, vol. 1, no. 1 (National Educational Closed-Circuit Television Association).

Raban, J.:
(1975) Review, *Radio Times*, 7 November (BBC Publications).

Williams, R.:
(1974) *Television: Technology and Cultural Form*, (Fontana).

1 Hall of mirrors

A favourite simile for television is the sheet of glass. The medium's chief attraction lies in its properties for revealing a panorama beyond our immediate horizon; for reflecting a world of possibilities that would otherwise be denied us. We are with reason often alarmed by the possibilities television conveys, and the medium itself is a common object of blame for the social problems it brings to light. But we know little of the ways in which television actually affects us. We assume that it does, for it certainly absorbs our time: but so, of course, does sleep, and during sleep some of the most gross distortions of all are prone to visit us. So what is television's impact? Does it actually have the all-pervasive role in our lives that has frequently been supposed? Or, like dreams, does it meet a psychological resistance that tells us the reflections are conjured? In this book we examine television's reflecting properties, we consider the intentions and techniques underlying the images it conveys, and also the ways in which its viewers attribute significance to the images they perceive. We also make a perhaps surprising but insistent point: that the subject matter conveyed by television is of less basic importance than is generally assumed; it is on the viewers' reactions to the imagery of television presentation that we must concentrate if the medium's fundamental psychological effects are to be established.

The transparent medium?

On 30 October 1936, the world's first public television service was launched from London's Alexandra Palace. The first evening of transmission featured a special BBC film, *Television comes to London*, to mark the historic occasion. The *Radio Times* — extended to include the new television schedule, and still known under its old name today — described the film as follows:

> [It gives] an idea of the growth of the television installation at Alexandra Palace and an insight into production routine. There will be many shots behind the scenes. One sequence, for instance, will show Adele Dixon as she appears to viewers in the Variety at 3.30

1

this afternoon, and will then reveal the technical staff and equipment in the studio that made this transmission possible. (Graham, 1974, p.14.)

It was doubtless of no surprise to the public of 1936 that the technology of television projected an image as potentially opaque as a scene in a theatre, behind which numerous unseen processes were operating. In revealing its behind the scenes secrets on the very first day of transmission, television also displayed a glorious ingenuousness. For what, at that stage, did its mysteries really consist of? In 1936, television was seen exclusively as 'a window on the world'. During the inaugural week, the TV programme schedule included concerts, a flower show, demonstrations of boxing, tap-dancing, and electronic music, though no actual use of the medium as an art form in its own right. Drama and ballet were featured, though each was relayed from one of the London theatres. The relative artlessness of television's own projection styles at that time represented a translucency that was soon to be lost as the art became more sophisticated. In the early days of television, enthusiasm for the medium's simple novelty generated production practices that today seem touchingly unadventurous. The evocative 'interlude' presentations, for example (*Waves on the Beach, Kittens at Play, Storm-tossed Clouds, The Potter's Wheel*): twenty years ago, these forms were acceptable (and, dare we say it, would be so again now — as the recent imitation of this form by certain British advertisers indicates). The medium *was* transparent. Its very transparency as a window on nature was exalted. But after the aesthetic value of a medium's simple novelty has declined, it must develop other means for reinstating itself in its audience's eyes. Gradually, the transparent medium of television became more opaque as the stylistic inventiveness of its users developed; and the course of this development is the same in all artistic media.

In the early days of film, the inventive play was even more apparent than it was in television. As a totally recorded medium, film is far more manipulate than its live counterpart, and the early work of the Meliés brothers in France at the turn of the century testifies to the boundless and magical possibilities that the medium was seen to offer. It is only in the 1970s that the electronics of television have become sufficiently sophisticated to compete on the 'special effects' market also. In celebration of the chroma-key technique alone (chapter 2) a fabulous style of documentary presentation has become possible in which musical works and the creative language of all of the arts are expressed in multiple images, freely fusing and dispersing. The potential of television as an art

2

form in its own right is now in the process of realisation; and since art is essentially the antithesis of transparency (witness the objections of some critics to pointillism as art), 'opaqueness' is now a necessary ingredient of TV stylistics as in any art form. (But consider our suggestion that a return to the simplicity of *Kittens at Play* might not be as unwelcome as one would think!)

Like any art, therefore, television is now skilled in the art of illusion. The skills of the producer, the actor, the film editor, the cameramen and engineers combine to create a product that will satisfy the criteria viewers have learned to apply to it. Occasionally, the behind the screen secrets of television production are partially revealed anew, as in such introspective programmes as the BBC's *Inside the News* and *Looking at Documentary* (both 1975) and *Film as Evidence* (1976): indeed, the recent intro-spectiveness of the British TV networks in this respect is an interesting feature of the current broadcasting climate, in which the Annan Committee is sitting to discuss the future of network television over the next few years. But although the techniques and mechanics of the medium are sometimes acknowledged, they are rarely allowed to become apparent in the creative act. Unless a particular style of media presentation is employed for an artistic effect in its own right (cf. the 'television vérité' styles discussed in the next chapter), the microphone and camera shadows are kept carefully out of the picture. For the medium to intrude upon the action is felt to destroy the illusion it creates. However, the presentation criteria that the medium applies in treating its material do not apply in the presentation of television's overtly artistic content alone. As television learned to emulate the traditional emphasis of the cinema upon constant variation of the image and the smooth continuity of its elements, those rules were applied in the presentation of drama and current affairs alike. The early criterion that newsreaders should be heard but not seen had, by the 1960s, given way to a norm by which they could not only be seen and heard but also identified by name. During the 1970s the television news on both sides of the Atlantic has been presented by two newsreaders per programme, alternating in the interests of visual appeal alone (chapter 2). Their appearance on the screen is buttressed by charts, photographs, filmed insert material (often with little relevance to the action reported), and gratuitous shots of the newsroom in which they work. The news is packaged and promoted like the soap operas and adverts that follow it; and the decision by a BBC news editor in 1976 to cut down on purely irrelevant packaging, even returning to a solo reader, has created as much interest on the part of the other news media as the news material they collectively convey: 'the news on

3

BBC TV is going to lose its trendy image . . . [dispensing with] many of the gimmicks that marked the presentation factors of news during the past year . . .' (*Daily Mail*, 19 February 1976).

The role of presentation in the television context may be seen as essentially similar to that of the elaborate non-verbal behaviour practised in communication situations generally (nods, smiles, eye movements, etc.). Like any mediating glass, television can distort and transform the material it presents by the way in which it presents it; and whilst it would be misleading to suggest that the non-transparency of a medium necessarily leads to dishonest reflections of its subject material, the means of presentation is certainly an important influence on the message's reception. Any message, in order to be communicated effectively by television or any other means, must be couched in terms that attract interest; and the techniques employed for this purpose in human communication generally are in no way exclusively verbal; without the underpinning of inflections, facial expression, posture and an elaborate routine of nods and non-verbal signals perfected through generations of practice, the immaculate verbal logic of an utterance is to no avail (cf. Argyle, 1969). As we shall see in chapter 3, an effective range of non-verbal skills is essential to the communication process, for by it the message stands or falls. In its absence, individuals are unable to form the basic human relationships from which communication stems; and in their attention to it, moreover, individuals are subject to the most unpredictable of prejudices.

The prejudicial ways in which a message may be interpreted are a central issue within this book. In normal conversation, our attitude to every word that is spoken is profoundly influenced by the relationships of trust and expectation by which the interaction is coloured; and if the figures that address us via television are to command our attention in the normal way, they must naturally be subject to the usual laws and conditions. On television, a succession of people claiming authority on one subject or another appears before us each day. If we have no prior knowledge of them, it is necessary for us to form an impression on whatever immediate basis we can: an impression as to whether they are sincere, humorous, and so on. For no-one likes to suspend judgement until the case has been argued: and, with the evidence of both eyes and ears, few can. When we speak, therefore, of a person's television 'image' we refer to a combination of ideas and predictions about that person which may actually vary according to the values we each apply. When we speak of a public image – either of an individual or of a cultural group – we imply that the audience's general reaction on the subject is united: and this indicates either some prior knowledge or a deliberate and powerful projection by the image makers. The image of a person, like a caricature, is a selection and amplification of certain features at the expense of others; and on television the nature of the impression a performer makes is potentially determined not merely by the performance itself but also, as we have indicated, by those who mediate it, by studio interviewers and by the complex television technology that the studio staff manipulates.

The extent to which television gives an actually dishonest reflection of the material it conveys is thus, in part at least, related to the intentions underlying the image building process. But distortions also occur when any aspect of the presentation is misinterpreted or gives rise to unwarranted assumptions. Not only is the performer's personal image liable to be deformed: the meaning of his spoken word may be misshapen to fit it. Whether it is formed consciously by the performer and his mediators, or assembled by the viewers according to their own criteria, the performer's media image may even determine the amount of basic attention paid to him. In ordinary human interaction, we accept that little of the speech passing between us fully registers. We may assume that others understand our own spoken intentions, but would admit that the attention we pay in return is usually less than perfect. Based on non-verbal skills alone, a satisfactory human exchange may occur with little concentration on what is actually spoken, and with the best of intentions two people can maintain the illusion of communication for hours. Though we accept this as a feature of face to face encounter, we forget it in our analyses of man and the media.

For media research has hitherto been based on the fatal assumption that a medium's influence may be analysed in terms of the effects of its subject matter alone. Media practitioners, on the other hand, realise that if visual presentation is neglected and the rich non-verbal code of cuts, fades and superimpositions is dispensed with, then audience attention will quite simply flag. The low esteem of much media research among media practitioners is thus hardly surprising. Emmett (1975) has summarised the broadcasters' often resentful attitude to media research in the following terms: their irritation with what they feel to be gratuitous advice, their annoyance at the frequent underestimation of their genuine concern for media development, and their scorn for the often elementary nature of research. But this is not to suggest that broadcasters scorn research *per se*: indeed, the major broadcasting organisations mount an expensive audience research effort (chapter 2). It is quite likely that focused specifically upon the effects of the production art itself, research techniques might reveal effects other than the producers have intuitively realised: and these, as

5

indicated by Robinson and Barnes (1976), actually would be of interest to them.

But if one's powers as a communicator are affected by the image that is presented, and if media presentation in turn is ruled by superficial criteria for simple variety, how much of televised content ever actually makes any impression? Previous research based on the analysis of subject matter alone has assumed that the latter comes over to its viewers in more or less pristine fashion. But does television actually speak to its audience with any more natural credibility than any other human agency? And does the audience really heed all of the information it imports? Or, like the man who plays the game of communication with us, does the medium fulfil most of our needs at a lower level than we like to imagine? We may imagine ourselves to be assimilating a programme's argument, only to realise, by the lack of any subsequent recollection of it, that we have happily spent the hour otherwise. Hearing our name spoken elsewhere in the room, we may recall the immediate context in which it occurred but have no recollection over the longer term. So content does go in, it seems, but swiftly decays unless we have reason to intellectualise it. And in our preoccupied state in front of the television set, it follows that the logical content of transmission may often be of less significance than the imagery that mediates it, the shadows and transitions of presentation alone.

In the chapters to follow this is our basic case. In the literature of television research evidence regarding presentation effects is sparse (Coldevin, 1976). Anderson (1972) reviews an abundance of 'non-significant' and inconsistent effects elicited when researchers have tried to compare the actual instructional effects of TV presentation (e.g. colour, motion, focal length, and lighting effects); and, admittedly on intuitive bases, he is led to suggest that research into the effects of presentation on attitude and interest levels may reveal a dimension on which the instructional gain from television is dependent. The educational programmes produced in the US by the Children's Television Workshop (Palmer, 1969) are accordingly based on the 'distractor theory' of TV education – the premise that the power to instruct depends on the ability to attract attention via presentation strategies specifically. Their classic series *Sesame Street* employs a wide range of studio and location techniques, music, humour, puppetry and graphic work to teach the principles of literacy and numeracy to children in the lower junior school range. (It is also hugely entertaining to adults.) *Sesame Street's* successor, *The Electric Company*, has been designed on the same principles, using, for instance, song and dance and sketch material with success, though it has achieved slower international sales. The third series from the CTW, also based on the distractor concept, has been *Feeling Good*, which provides instruction on personal health for adults. This, however, has been the least popular of the CTW products, though the reasons that the series does not 'feel so good' as the others are not readily apparent (Palmer, 1976). What the effects of these series do probably show however, is the dynamic development not only of TV techniques but also of audience responses to them: a well-principled technique is only effective for so long before the audience itself becomes sophisticated in its response to the genre and demands something a little different.

The literature of the cinema, with a far longer history, has been deeply aware of this and in film analysis the questions of direction and artistic technique are uppermost (Wollen, 1969). The order and context in which particular shots and slices of the action are presented has long been known to be of prime importance in the manner in which it is interpreted (Eisenstein, 1947); and Isenhour (1975) reviews a collection of experiments conducted by Eisenstein and other pioneers of film direction and analysis such as Goldberg (1951) and Pudovkin (1958). The Kuleshov–Pudovkin effect reported by Pudovkin indicates that a neutral shot will be interpreted in dramatically opposite terms according to the shots with which it is juxtaposed: thus an expressionless face seems either happy, pensive or sad according to the shot by which it is preceded (e.g. a little girl playing, a bowl of soup, or a dead woman in a coffin). Whether any material conveyed by the visual media can ever appear totally unambiguous is therefore extremely debatable. Some writers on film, notably Bazin and Barthes (also cited by Wollen, 1969) have maintained that a clear expression of its intended meaning is possible, and that the intentions of a medium to reflect 'real events' and scenarios can thus be transparent; but in the chapters to follow we argue that this is only the case if the audience is well-versed in how to interpret the medium by a process akin to visual literacy – and, moreover, if it has the opportunity to check its interpretations. It is a conclusion to which we have been led by the data we have observed, both experimentally and from previous writings. We conclude that the 'transparency of the medium', as often upheld, is a myth put about by those who do not appreciate its psychological subtleties. A variant on the same myth supposes that freedom of access to the medium (chapter 6) will effectively demystify its subtleties, rendering it once again as transparent as the day it was born. We argue, however, that the basic properties of television relate to no fixed and finite set of factors but to the dynamic psychological processes whereby its content is construed. We suggest that in educational use, for example, an understanding of these processes may be harnessed in the

7

interests of greater control over the medium's informative properties in future; and in chapter 7 of the book we examine the future telecommunications contexts by which the dynamics of television will be further shaped.

Traditional theories of communication, however, provide little clue as to either the psychological properties of media or the possibilities for their more controlled usage. In the following section we therefore examine traditional models of communication and relate them to the views held by philosophers of man the perceiver of the world around him.

'Signal' and 'noise'

The purpose of communication theorists (cf. Lin, 1973) has been to define the processes involved when a signal, or message, passes from its source to an independent system with facilities for signal detection. At the simplest level of understanding, the communication act may be described as in Fig. 1.1, where 'to communicate' is seen exclusively as the act of the message sender, while the recipients, totally passive, merely receive. In 1949, however, the model was described rather more precisely by Shannon and Weaver; by direct analogy to the electrical engineering model of communication, they added to the basic view components of message transmission and decoding (see Fig. 1.2). In this model the recipient is less docile: on leaving its source, a message is conveyed in coded form as a signal to a system capable of deciphering it. Within the channel used, however, communication may be impeded by interference with the signal, by 'noise': thus the communication process is acknowledged to be fallible.

But the model is still deficient. The origins of 'noise', for example, remain inexplicit; moreover, as indication that it has been communicated successfully, the independent system's fidelity to the signal in relaying it must be examined. Only then is the extent to which communication has taken place to the required degree strictly apparent — for it may emerge from this analysis that the transmission of the message has been influenced by 'noise' factors not previously taken into account.

A more explicit version of the Shannon and Weaver model is thus presented by Fig. 1.3. The communication linking two participant systems is seen as a circuit, in which a message is dispatched from its source, coded, transmitted, received, decoded, and ultimately relayed by the same process. The destination of the initial message becomes in its turn the new source for its relay; and the measure of communication is the extent to which, despite the impingeing noise within the system, the message can be

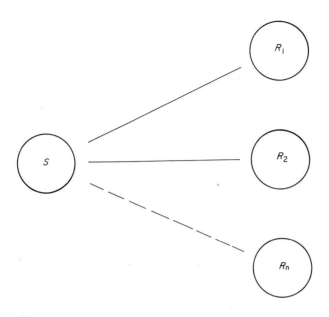

Fig. 1.1   The communication process: simple model

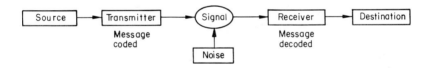

Fig. 1.2   Shannon and Weaver's (1949) communication model

returned to its original source in its original form. The main advantage of
this expression of the process over the traditional engineering model is
that noise factors are recognised as arising at any stage in the circuit and
not simply from some external agency. Several theorists have emphasised
the fallibility of human communication, placing different stress on its
origins at various stages of the process. Burke (1945) indicates the
complexity of the human transmission process in communication, and the
effects of the message sender's underlying motivation. Lasswell (1948)
defines the variables underlying communication more fully as 'who says
what in what channel to whom with what effect?'; while other writers
(e.g. Riley and Riley, 1959; Secord and Backman, 1974) stress the

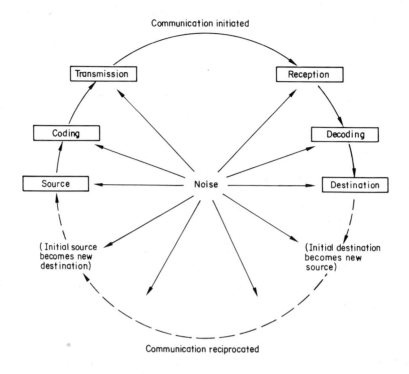

Fig. 1.3   The communication circuit

dependency of the communication process on the social system in which it occurs. Our control of communication processes depends on the extent to which all of these extraneous effects in their various forms can be identified and minimised. In our analysis of effects arising when a message is mediated via television, therefore, we seek to distinguish signal from noise not only in the nature of the source and the coded form in which the message is expressed (chapter 2), but also in the viewer's receptive capacity, and the logic used when the message is decoded (chapters 3 and 4). The effects of 'noise' may never be cancelled entirely, though, since as one's capacity for separating the noise from the signal increases, so the more severe problems of communication in a given medium can be avoided.

In electronic systems of communication, the cause and effects of noise can now be controlled with some sophistication. But since noise factors in human communication processes are not merely technical but also psychological in origin, our control over these is more limited. We need to identify the dynamic effects of attitude and experience on the ways in which the human system attributes meaning to the message it receives, meaning that may never be explicit solely in the form a message takes on re-transmission. We must also recognise, however, as in the previous section, that the mediated form a message takes may in fact provide the only definition of its content there is: that little intended meaning may actually underlie it. And in view of these problems, a theorist might be forgiven for doubting whether any clearcut definition of the communication process is ever possible!

This thought has often occurred to philosophers. A fundamental question of interest within philosophical theory has been that of human perceptual ability, without which little successful adaptation to the environment is possible, and certainly none of the two-way communicative type. The question has been posed in two traditional forms:

(1) What are the actual practical *mechanisms* that man employs in perceiving the world around him? and
(2) What is perception? Can man ever, in fact, really know what he perceives at all?

Before coming to be identified with distinct traditions within psychology and philosophy specifically, these two forms of the question were classified as *physical* and *metaphysical.* A problem illustrating the two approaches is that of visual depth perception (Boring, 1942). To the early philosophers the puzzle was in understanding how an object may be seen as three-dimensional even though the image of that object on the retina is two-dimensional. Until the seventeenth century, the basic theory of the physicists in this respect was that an object's distance is perceived strictly according to the invisible angles at which light waves from an object converge upon the two eyes separately. The British empiricist school of philosophers in the seventeenth and eighteenth centuries espoused the notion of the physicists that all knowledge derives purely from the senses in this way. Locke indicated that the senses convey to us information about an object, some of which accurately represents the reality of the object and the rest of which does not. Berkeley went a stage further than this, and was more realistic than Locke, by pointing out that we never can know for certain the extent to which this is so — the extent to which the real world and our mental images of the real world coincide — for we only have our mental images to go on. So saying, he in effect restated the argument put forward by Plato in the fourth century BC that nothing in the world around us is *really* real at all. To Plato the world of phenomena is a poor reflection from another ideal world; in his theory of forms he

11

offers the 'cave analogy' which suggests that man exists within the confines of a cave into which the *real* world casts shadows. All that we can perceive is a reflection, an interpretation of reality as in a mirror. (The mirror is thus our opaque medium, and the effects of the world upon us can only be understood in terms of the ways in which we interpret it.) The idea is reiterated by the modern philosopher Popper (1963), who cautions us that, while as scientists we may search for the truth, it will always ultimately elude us: 'for all is but a woven web of guesses'.

The cave analogy is at once a great statement of the fallibility of human processes and of their psychological complexity. It counsels a modest realisation of our inability ever to formulate the final answers to our questions; but it indicates that the most satisfactory answers may nonetheless be sought from several different directions at once. The processes of human perception, and thence communication, may be studied by an examination of the mind's interpretative processes in a variety of ways; and Berkeley's contribution to the problem of visual depth perception was to consider the dynamic ways in which the mind *organises* the material the senses convey to it accordingly. For, asked Berkeley, if the perception of depth depends upon the simultaneous agency of both eyes at once, what about the one-eyed man? He can perceive the three-dimensional properties of the world despite his disability, so the strictly physical theory about light waves and angles must be inadequate. In part at least, the mind must interpret what it perceives according to the ways it has *learned* to do so (see chapter 3).

Within twentieth century psychology, the different ways in which individuals interpret their world have been emphasised in numerous behavioural contexts. Bartlett (1932) spoke of the set of psychological *schemata* governing individual behaviour; Gregory (1970) has referred to the process by which information is judged in relation to a set of *internal models.* Kelly (1955), on the other hand, has propounded a theory of *personal constructs*, indicating that man views (construes) the world according to his own characteristic set of psychological criteria. Taken at this level, of course, such theoretical notions merely duplicate those for which the Greeks also had a word, when they referred to mental *traces.* But, in fact, Kelly's theory goes further than merely describing: it aims to understand the process by which man relates his percepts to his behaviour in everyday life. Man in general, argues Kelly, uses the rational approach of a scientist in viewing the world, gathering evidence about it, forming hypotheses and testing them out. Constantly relating observations to his repertoire of personal constructs, he analyses the complex interaction of variables that he perceives and thereby comes to terms with the environment in which he must function. Any process by which one item of information is related to another, Kelly indicates, involves their comparison for similarities and differences; and in Kelly's personal construct theory the analysis of incoming data is seen explicitly in these terms. The theory provides us with an insight into man's psychological processes which is independent of the type of determinist assumption that has mitigated against psychological theory in the past (chapter 2). Moreover, it has generated an empirical tool, the repertory grid technique, whose use in a non-determinist study of man's reactions to the television medium will be indicated in chapters 2 and 6.

The philosophers' view of human perception as a glimpse, through a clouded medium, at absolutes that may never be defined can set our mind at rest as to whether we shall ever understand the total impact of external forces on human cognition *in vacuo*. Yet previous attempts at the analysis of the media's impact via definitions of its subject matter seem to have assumed that this is possible. In the total framework of research into television's effects, an analysis of subject matter is an indispensable element; but equally indispensable is the role of he who receives it, the viewer. In the impersonal nature of the broadcast medium at present, unfortunately, the viewer's role in the process is rather more assumed than it is known. (Only in a two-way communication system is it actually made plain.) But, as we shall attempt to show, it makes little sense even so to study the medium in terms of its message input alone. Even if a strict analysis of the television message were possible we should see that its journey from source to destination takes it through a hall of mirrors with numerous dynamic properties for dissolving and reconstituting the meaning it conveys.

Media dynamics

The rest of the book therefore describes a dynamic approach to the understanding of television's properties which is designed to avoid some of the assumptions made in previous investigations. The essence of dynamism is change; and a question as many-sided as the impact of television demands an approach that caters both for the changes that take place within the medium itself — on the part of those who design its content — and for those on the viewers' part that determine its final effects. Thus we examine the shifting criteria underlying the production of the television image, the psychodynamic factors determining the viewing experience, and the extent to which, despite all this flux, the effects of television can be identified and controlled. Central to each aspect of the question is the 'television message', concerning which the biggest assumptions of all have been made hitherto. In view of the total flux apparent at every level of the human communication process, the communicated message is the very element that cannot be defined *a priori.* We may assume the nature of the message for simple descriptive reasons, but may base no conclusions about its cause or effects upon these assumptions. Moreover, if we wish to predict the effects of a particular message on another occasion, on another audience, and in another context, we must be prepared to find that our existing description no longer obtains.

Our initial frames of reference, then, must be capable of revision and even rejection according to the situation and the moment under analysis. The descriptive approach we adopt must avoid any assumption that the properties of television are ever discrete and finite — we must also avoid all labels that in themselves attempt to pin down the phenomena of the medium too fixedly. We must look not merely at the phenomena themselves but for the forces behind them. By observing the relationships between the various reference points we use, however, we may ultimately come to understand the dynamics of television and be able to predict them.

It is for the rest of the book to show what these dynamics may be. In chapter 2 we examine the particular problems of the content analytic approach to television, the partial extent to which it may prove useful as the only approach to the medium's effects, and a number of factors which prevent it from ever being conclusive.

Summary

(1)   Television has been seen as a medium capable of reflecting the world at different levels of accuracy. The role of presentation in the communication of a message, however, invariably affects its impact; and the over-emphasis of previous research on the effects of television's overt subject matter needs redressing.

(2)   Models of the communication process, attempting to define its variability in terms of static 'noise' factors, inadequately reflect its psychological complexity. Ancient and modern philosophers remind us that psychological capacities are essentially fallible and determined by the dynamic processes of organisation and experience.

(3)   In order to understand the effects of television we must examine its dynamic properties via an appropriately flexible approach.

References

Anderson, C. M. (1972), 'In search of a visual rhetoric for instructional television', *AV Communication Review*, vol. 20, no. 1.

Argyle, M. (1969), *Social Interaction*, London, Methuen.

Bartlett, F. (1932), *Remembering*, Cambridge, Cambridge University Press.

Berkeley, G. (ed. D. Armstrong), *Berkeley's Philosophical Writings*, London, Collier Macmillan, 1965.

Boring, E. G. (1942), *Sensation and Perception in the History of Experimental Psychology*, New York, Appleton-Century-Crofts.

Burke, K. (1945), *A Grammar of Motives*, New Jersey, Prentice-Hall.

Coldevin, G. (1976), 'Comparative effectiveness of ETV presentation variables', *Journal of Educational Television*, vol. 2, no. 3.

Eisenstein, S. M. (1947), *The Film Sense*, New York, Harcourt and Brace.

Emmett, B. (1975), 'The perspective of the broadcaster', paper read to the Conference of the British Psychological Society (Social Section), University College, London.

Goldberg, H. D. (1951), 'The role of "cutting" in the perception of the motion picture', *Journal of Applied Psychology*, vol. 35.

Graham, B. (1974), *Television*, London, Marshall Cavendish.

Gregory, R. L. (1970), 'On how so little information controls so much behaviour', *Ergonomics*, vol. 13.

Isenhour, J. P. (1975), 'The effects of context and order in film editing', *AV Communication Review*, vol. 23, no. 1.

Kelly, G. A. (1955), *The Psychology of Personal Constructs*, New York, Norton.

Lasswell, H. D. (1948), 'The structure and function of communication', in Bryson, L. (ed.), *The Communication of Ideas*, New York, Harper.

Lin, N. (1973), *The Study of Human Communication*, New York, Bobbs-Merrill.

Locke, J. (ed. A. C. Fraser), *An Essay Concerning Human Understanding*, New York, Dover Publications, 1959.

Palmer, E. L. (1969), 'Research at the Children's Television Workshop', *Educational Broadcasting Review*, vol. 3, no. 5.

Palmer, E. L. (1976), keynote address to the International Conference on Evaluation and Research in Educational Broadcasting, Open University.

Popper, Sir K. (1963), *Conjectures and Refutations: the Growth of Scientific Knowledge*, London, Routledge and Kegan Paul.

Pudovkin, V. I. (1958), *Film Technique and Film Acting*, London, Vision Press.

Riley, J. W., Jr and Riley, M. W. (1959), 'Mass communication and the social system', in Merton, R. K., Broom, L. and Cottrell, L. S. (eds), *Sociology Today: Problems and Prospects*, New York, Basic Books.

Robinson, J. and Barnes, N. (1976), 'Evaluation in adult education broadcasting?', *Journal of Educational Television,* vol. 2, no. 3.

Secord, P. and Backman, C. W. (1974), *Social Psychology*, New York, McGraw-Hill.

Shannon, C. E. and Weaver, W. (1949), *The Mathematical Theory of Communication*, Urbana, University of Illinois Press.

Wollen, P. (1969), *Signs and Meaning in the Cinema*, London, Secker and Warburg.

2 Analysis of the TV message

The content of TV programmes amounts to a complex set of messages put out by a producer and his team for the viewer to receive. It is clearly necessary for us to examine both of these facets: not only the structure and declared content of the TV message itself but also the processes underlying the viewing experience. More emphasis has traditionally been placed on the first of these two parts, to the virtual exclusion of the second, and whilst our analysis and supporting experimental evidence later in the book will bear mainly on the neglected second element, it makes logical and historical sense to consider the producer's message and intentions first. The present chapter will show ways in which this traditional emphasis fails to account adequately for viewers' responses, and in the next we shall begin to look at the dynamic processes underlying the viewers' responses specifically.

Analysis of the TV message begins, as does any psychological enquiry, with the naming of parts. Previous investigations of TV's effects, interpreting its psychological role in terms of sociological factors, and 'the mass', have emphasised the specific effects of its thematic content: violence on TV, educational material on TV, news and current affairs programmes on TV. Each of these has been the focal point for an enormous amount of specialist research and, in its turn, subdivision. The ultimate concern of previous research in general has been to monitor and forewarn of the effects of thematic content upon those sectors of the population at which it is directed; and the grounding of this work in the determinist tradition discussed earlier is explicit. Our own work, however, is concerned less with the overt effects of media subject matter than with the stylistics of its presentation; and thus recognises the analysis of thematic elements as only one feature of a far more complicated problem. As it is naturally an important feature we shall concentrate initially on the dominant thematic characteristics of TV content, at the broad programme by programme level in which messages are grouped. The conventional approach to content analysis, however, leads directly to questions about a programme's *function*: and this presents us with another criterion for the analysis of message content. As our argument develops, during the present chapter specifically and the remainder of the book in general, we shall focus attention upon more fundamental issues of message technique and style: for in these the dynamics of television are observed at their strongest.

Traditional analytical criteria

The traditional emphasis on thematic groupings in TV content has been problematic at its very roots. Even the search for a basic taxonomy of programme types is frustrated by the virtual certainty that even in a specific programme several generic characteristics (e.g. adventure, comedy, romance, etc.) will probably overlap. The problem attends analyses of genre in all creative media, preventing any systematic study of their dynamic properties. In television research — particularly in view of the concern with which the medium's potential effects are viewed — the lack of an effective programme typology has been especially unfortunate: for the need to define television's impact is felt at numerous levels, both theoretical and applied. For example, the major broadcasting organisations conduct elaborate and continuous audience research for the express purpose of improving and developing their service. The basic evaluative method (an after the event assessment of programme effects by, for example, a simple viewing tally or audience appreciation ratings) provides, for those who produce the material, the only statistical 'knowledge of results' presently available. Such feedback is speedy and relatively specific, showing, for example, that a certain proportion of the estimated audience for a given programme evidently enjoyed it while the remainder did not. More detailed information (on particular aspects of the programme, or on sex, age, and social class differences within the audience) may also be given. Yet such feedback has very little predictive value. For the programmer or media researcher anxious for information as to the likely effects of a particular programme genre, any extrapolation from specific data is a matter for caution.

In fact, even the major audience research organisations pay scant attention to problems of genre, being content to classify TV output on a simple programme by programme basis within the weekly cycle, and creating groupings by purely *ad hoc* criteria. In view of the continual flux and change of media forms on the dynamic basis discussed in chapter 1, this approach is understandable — but it does limit the credibility of audience research conclusions. Dannheisser (1975) reports a typical breakdown, by the Independent Broadcasting Authority's Audience Research Department, of viewers' appreciation data across eight programme categories from 'adventure' to 'miscellaneous'. In the comedy/

light entertainment category is included the quiz game *University Challenge* and the personality biography *This is Your Life*. The two are presumably grouped this way by virtue of their light entertainment characteristic; but both are far removed from comedy and make disparate bedfellows. Similarly, under 'romance series' the daily life serials *General Hospital* and *Coronation Street* are subsumed, neither of which notably emphasises the romantic element. In a rider to his report, Dannheisser emphasises that comparisons of audience appreciation scores *across* different programme categories are not valid; but it would surely be equally rash to make them *within*.

A more effective classification system has been developed by Williams (1974). Based in the main on conventional departmental divisions within the broadcasting organisations, twelve basic output types are distinguished as follows: news and public affairs; features and documentaries; education; arts and music; children's programmes; drama; movies; general entertainment; sport; religion; publicity (internal); and commercials. These categories still contain many overlaps, as Williams indicates, but in the context of his discussions of programme scheduling strategy and the various programme subtypes, the categories he proposes prove a useful analytical base, as evinced subsequently by Goodhardt et al. (1975) in their investigation of viewing patterns for the Independent Broadcasting Authority. Much of the overlap within Williams' system may actually be resolved, for what has been overlooked in such studies is the basic analytic maxim of Lasswell (1948): namely, that communication analysts must concern themselves with the separate questions of 'who says what in what channel to whom, and with what effect?'

In the analysis of programme type at the traditional broad level, the 'how?' (in what channel?) and 'who?' are dealt with in passing, as being respectively the technology under discussion and the trained professionals that use it: we shall do likewise for the moment, reconsidering each at appropriate stages in the discussion to follow. The question 'what?' refers to the messages conveyed, and 'with what effect?' is the riddle of the viewing experience at which the analysis aims ultimately. 'To whom?' in the present connection proves problematic. We may define the audience for which a programme is intended: Williams' taxonomy includes children's programmes as a significant expression of intention in this manner. Yet children's programmes are certainly not exclusively viewed by children — the puppet cartoon *The Magic Roundabout*, transmitted on BBC-1 immediately before the early evening news, is a notably adult favourite. Equally, children do not watch only those programmes intended for them: Wober (1975) illustrates the simple truth that from the earliest ages children view and recall a substantial proportion of programmes intended for adults, and from the ages of eight to eleven upwards may even prefer them. In the analysis of actual message types, therefore, the criterion of audience is too vague to be of any fundamental value. In a sociological study of the media, where group homogeneity is emphasised for the purpose of eliciting broad effects differentiating social groups, audience definitions can be more meaningful. But in the psychological study of TV's impact, viewers' individual characteristics are the least known quantities of all, and attempts to assume them in the absence of specific information are theoretically inhibiting.

In conventional analyses of programme content, unfortunately, categories defining its thematic characteristics and its intended audience have been confounded. Even mediating technique − the 'how?' of a medium's usage − has been implicated by the general references to, for example, drama, movies, and the documentary. In fact, each commonly reflects a more fundamental criterion already hinted at, that of the programme's *purpose*: this Lasswell does not acknowledge, though Burke (1945) had regarded it as a central aspect of the communication process. The most basic relationship in programme content emerges as that between its purpose and its theme. At one level of definition, the theme and purpose of a programme are separate issues entirely. While arts and music, and sport (cf. Williams, 1974) are unambiguous thematic categories, education is a label applied to programmes on innumerable themes and addressed to diverse types of audience; and unless the theme of an educational programme is an actual area of educational method or policy itself, this classification indicates a purposive intention and is not thematic at all. But in practical analysis, the relationship of theme and purpose actually proves sufficiently stable for close examination, and provides a more reliable base for analyses of programme type than any of the other criteria examined so far. The basic question − to be treated in the next section − is thus the joint one 'what is said on television and why?'

Theme and intended function

A definition of his programme's purpose − the function for which it is intended − is one that no broadcaster at any rate would shirk. The clear and declared function of educational, and news and public affairs programmes, is naturally to inform, the most basic of all media functions. The internal publicity announcements of a TV channel regarding, for example, programmes for transmission later, also have an informative function, no less than the commercials that accompany them. The informative manner of the latter, of course, is emotionally clouded by dint of their being considered 'persuasive' (a point taken up in more detail in chapter 5). Attributing to advertisers other than altruistic motives, we may overlook that to all intents the functions of persuasion and instruction are indistinguishable, for the intention to influence future attitudes and actions via carefully instilled principles is common to both advertisements and informational programmes. The separate ideological motives of an educational and a propagandist TV programme may be debatable, but the intended function of both is nonetheless to be informative with respect to the ideology in question. On the basis of function we may now begin to classify certain of the conventional programme types more rigorously. In addition to the educational, commercial, and news/public affairs categories, we may bracket in the basically informative class programmes dealing with religious and sundry campaigning themes (politics, social issues, fundraising, etc.). Internal publicity belongs in this class equally: though this we shall rename continuity in order to accommodate those other aspects of viewing content (test cards, station call signs, etc.) by which the gaps in programme content are filled. In order to combine them under the same heading as news programmes, we shall limit the subcategory public affairs in Williams' analysis to current affairs since public affairs are dealt with in various functional guises (e.g. educational and campaigning): material in the composite category news and current affairs is thereby primarily characterised by its topicality.

For an appropriate set of thematic categories describing the medium's other basic function (entertainment) we must inspect the range of television 'entertainment' shows for areas of correspondence. Adventure, mystery, crime, horror: all are recognisable genres in their own right, but for the sake of economy they may in the present analysis be classified as thriller themes by virtue of their mutual emphasis on action and suspense. Two categories easily defined are romance and humour, both capable of overlap but each a popular thematic type likely to be dominant in a significant proportion of entertainment programmes. To humour must be added its antonym pathos, a possible concomitant of, for example, the romance element, though capable of serving a thematic function in its own right. Other popular themes — daily life (as in the *Crossroads* or *Coronation Street* type of serial), boardroom intrigue (as in *The Power Game* and *The Brothers*) animal stories, school yarns, science fiction, and innumerable other specific one-off themes — may be classified, perhaps unsatisfactorily, as general interest themes. (Each of these sub-themes may of course be specifically considered in future analyses if so required.) To the five major categories we may add the musical variety component of Williams' general entertainment category, in which a sequence of song, dance, and/or novelty items is featured; and with the addition of four intermediate categories, none of which falls neatly into the informative or entertainment classes of programme *per se*, the list may be considered complete.

These four latter categories in our system are: sports and pastimes; games and quiz shows; personality shows (concerning specific persons) and aesthetics (a category subsuming the cultural arts). Sports and pastimes, dealing with all aspects of indoor and outdoor leisure pursuit except those specifically generic to the television studio, is described as fulfilling a combined 'entertainment as information' function ('E as I'). Material within any entertainment category may qualify as serving an information function from time to time, though sports information is the prime 'E as I' example, being produced with sufficient regularity to warrant its transmission in special sports news allocations. Even though presented after the style of programmes with a specifically informative brief, the informative function of sports output is nonetheless subordinate to that of entertainment, hence its 'E as I' definition. Games and quiz shows on the other hand (e.g. *Mastermind; University Challenge* and *Double Your Money*) fulfil the converse function of 'information as entertainment' ('I as E') and in the examples given both for this function and for that of 'E as I', the entertainment value springs from the competitive element. Also fulfilling the 'I as E' function, however, is the type of programme in which information about specific people is presented for an entertainment purpose (e.g. *This is Your Life*, and the various 'talk shows'): this category we may term personality. (On American channels show-business/personality information receives special 'news' allocations as does sports.)

The final category into which a sizeable amount of TV material falls is described as aesthetics, one whose entertainment and information functions are indistinguishable. Programmes in this category ('E = I') are thematically linked by their treatment of topics such as sculpture, music, and the other cultural forms, and they may feasibly include analyses of any of the thematic types already discussed: the theatre, cinema, even television itself may form a subject for stylistic analysis within the aesthetics genre in this way.

As emphasised previously, in specific programme contents all generic categories may overlap; such interaction may be either sequential or simultaneous. It is the thesis of later sections in this chapter that no aspect of TV content is ever capable of definition on a taxonomic basis exclusively; though certain broad research questions may be served by generic systems as long as several message dimensions (function, theme, etc.) are not confounded as one. The sixteen thematic elements of TV content are therefore summarised in Table 2.1. In all types of message, as

Table 2.1

Functional and thematic aspects of TV content

Function	Informative	Entertainment
Theme	News and current affairs	Thriller
		Romance
	Educational	General interest
	Religious	Humour
	Campaigning	Pathos
	Commercial	Musical variety
	Continuity	('I as E'): personality
	('E as I'): sports and pastimes	('I as E'): games and quiz shows
	('I = E'): aesthetics	

in any normal communication systems generally, intended function and theme are complementary. If they come into conflict, as in certain pathological states known technically as 'double-bind' (Bateson, 1973), where one thing is said though another signified, the system breaks down. In social situations such breakdown is avoided by the existence of group codes and controls: the public broadcasting media, for example, are restricted to the entertainment and information functions in order to prevent their use as agents of social unrest. Within the prevailing ideology, other functions — for example, shocking without informative intent — are regarded as permissive. As the bounds of permissiveness are redefined, and new conventional criteria for media usage continually emerge, permissive intentions are themselves subsumed under an informative or entertainment heading. In terms of basic intention, the functional–thematic rationale is thus quite stable. And even though the reflection of television's properties it provides is greatly restricted, the rationale nevertheless permits an examination of several of the medium's broad output characteristics.

Programme schedule analysis

The most general questions concerning television's output are those faced in the planning of programme schedules, channel by channel, at a broad week by week level. Typically: is there adequate balance between the educational and entertainment content? Similarly: are the needs of minority audiences fairly catered for? It is the intention of broadcasting policy to ensure that an appropriate weekly balance is maintained, both between and within channels, in these respects. Whether this intention is satisfactorily realised over longer periods is one of the areas of traditional audience research. Rowley (1975), for instance, reports the gradual changes in programme balance within the ITV companies' schedules during the period 1970–75: increasing proportions of 'serious' programmes and narrative material are observed – also the development of programmes with a regional theme. As in other analyses, the questions of audience, function, theme and technique, however, are confounded.

In order to examine the types of programme content more precisely, let us therefore extricate the separate message dimensions as distinct criteria by which to define them. On the basis of function and theme alone, the extent to which programmers' intentions regarding balance are reflected in the overt weekly output may be checked quite satisfactorily as in analyses 1–4 below. (For a check on the balance in material intended for particular viewing audiences the latter must be defined *a priori*, and programmes categorised according to function and theme in that specific light.)

(1) An illustration of the approach is provided by an analysis of published BBC- and Granada-TV schedules for the week beginning 28 February 1976. The schedule items were each allocated by three judges to one of the generic categories given in Table 2.1 above. (Details of commercial and continuity content are not of course published, and at this level of analysis are not therefore recorded.) The judgements were based first on the question of the item's intended function (entertainment or information?) and on the thematic question accordingly. In the event

of an apparent overlap between several categories, the judges were instructed to decide which category predominantly represented the programme's function and theme.

The comparison of their responses indicated the judges to be in agreement as to the correct category to which 97 per cent of the programmes should be allocated. The 3 per cent disagreement occurred predominantly over the decisions as to whether programmes should be described as:

(a) *General interest*, or *humour*: children's programmes in particular, as we have observed earlier in the chapter, present particular definition problems in this respect. Content that seems humorous to an adult may certainly not be so to a child, and the majority of disagreements between these two categories accordingly occurred in relation to children's programmes (e.g. cartoons and puppetry). Unless the humorous element in a programme was obviously dominant (as in *Tom and Jerry*, and *The Flintstones*), it was eventually classified as an item of general interest.

(b) *General interest*, or *thriller*: a few programmes (e.g. *The Adventures of Black Beauty*, and *The Brothers*) were classified by judges under both headings, and in event of doubt as to their status as thrillers were classified as general interest as in (a) above.

(c) *Educational*, or *sports and pastimes*: several judges tended to classify programmes concerning, for example, cookery (*The Galloping Gourmet*), and painting (*Paint Along with Nancy*) as educational. In these instances disagreement between judges was easily resolved by classifying them as concerning pastimes. Other disagreements – as to which of the two categories children's programmes such as *Magpie* and *Rainbow* belong to – are less easy to resolve. In the event these have ultimately been classified as educational in view of the overt intention in broadcasting policy that such programmes should have a primarily educational function (cf. Howitt and Cumberbatch, 1976).

In their allocation of schedule items to all other thematic categories the judges were concordant. The proportional representation of each category is given for the three TV channels in Fig. 2.1.

(2) A second, identical analysis was performed for the following week (beginning 6 March 1976). Three different judges were enlisted, and agreement between them was slightly lower at 94 per cent; as before, disagreement between them mainly occurred in relation to the general interest/humour/thriller, and educational/sports and pastimes categories.

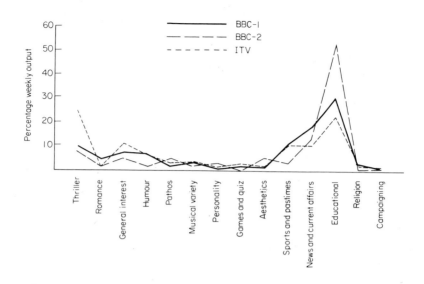

Fig. 2.1   Schedule analysis: proportional representation of each thematic category (week commencing 28 February 1976)

The thematic balance of them in this schedule is virtually identical to that in the first analysis shown above (cf. the results of product–moment correlation analyses given in Table 2.2).

Table 2.2

Schedule analysis: Pearson product–moment correlations between weeks commencing 28 February and 6 March 1976

BBC-1	BBC-2	ITV
$r = 0.98$	$r = 0.99$	$r = 0.97$
$t = 16.97$	$t = 24.46$	$t = 13.02$
$p < 0.001$	$p < 0.001$	$p < 0.001$

(3)   The *average* allocations for the two-week period 28 February to 12 March 1976 were compared with an analysis for the Christmas holiday week beginning 22 December 1975. A further three judges were employed to allocate each item in the Christmas programme schedule to one of the

fourteen thematic categories as before. Their judgements were concordant with respect to 96 per cent of the programmes, the only notable conflict being between general interest and humour classifications (naturally higher than usual in the festive period). In Figs 2.2 to 2.4 the estimates of normal programming balance and those referring to the holiday period are compared for each channel. The results of product–moment correlations between normal and festive programmes in each channel are appended to the appropriate figure.

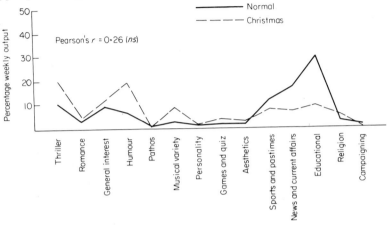

Fig. 2.2   Normal and Christmas week programme schedules compared –
BBC-1

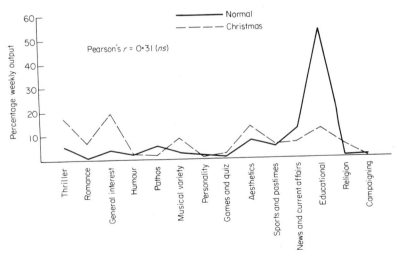

Fig. 2.3   Normal and Christmas week programme schedules compared –
BBC-2

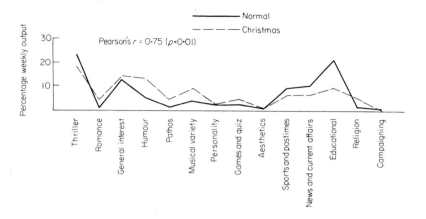

Fig. 2.4 Normal and Christmas week programme schedules compared —
ITV

During the rarity periods such as a Christmas or Bank Holiday week, schedule planners clearly develop distinctive intentions in their need to cater for a more intensive viewing demand than is customary. In the above analyses, the thematic proportions in normal and festive programmes scheduled by the BBC channels show a predictably non-significant correlation, though (interestingly enough) the normal and Christmas ITV programmes are seen to be significantly similar. Of course, the ITV channel, which carries more entertainment material than either of the other two all the year round, has an especial problem in making its fare seem extra-festive to suit the Christmas mood. This, in fact, all the channels do by the simple festive packaging of their programmes in the continuity slots and TV publications: quite ordinary (non-festive) material is 'dressed-up' with a new title (*Christmas with Kojak, Christmas with Bogart* etc.) to give them a semblance of being season-specific which is actually quite bogus.

The data from each of the above schedule analyses are collated in Table 2.3. As a whole they describe a more reliable approach — by the classification of output according to function and theme alone — to the general questions of schedule balance than is adopted conventionally. As we have seen earlier, the functions of communication in a well-ordered society (to entertain or to inform) remain constant; and in the analysis of messages transmitted via television, it is generally the question of function

Table 2.3

Schedule analysis: % proportions of weekly output time in each thematic category

	BBC-1			BBC-2			ITV			Marginal overlaps (<1% total programmes)
	Normal week 1	Normal week 2	Christmas week	Normal week 1	Normal week 2	Christmas week	Normal week 1	Normal week 2	Christmas week	
Entertainment function										
Thriller	9·6	11·1	20·0	6·7	4·0	17·0	24·1	23·6	18·1	with 3
Romance	4·4	1·7	4·3	1·6	0·1	6·7	1·4	1·4	4·1	with 1 + 4
General interest	7·6	11·9	11·7	4·7	2·7	18·7	10·9	15·7	14·4	with 3
Humour	6·1	6·1	19·1	1·6	2·3	2·0	6·1	5·0	13·6	
Pathos	1·7	0·0	0·4	4·7	5·6	1·9	2·3	1·3	4·3	
Musical variety	2·9	2·0	8·7	1·9	2·4	8·4	3·3	4·9	9·4	
I as E										
Personality	0·6	1·3	1·9	2·3	0·0	1·0	1·4	2·7	2·9	
Games and quiz	1·9	1·3	3·6	0·0	1·3	2·0	2·6	2·1	4·3	
E = I										
Aesthetics	1·3	1·9	2·4	5·0	0·3	12·7	1·7	0·4	0·9	
E as I										
Sports and pastimes	11·4	11·1	7·4	3·3	5·4	5·9	10·4	8·3	6·1	with 12
Informative function										
News and current affairs	18·4	19·3	6·6	13·9	11·3	6·7	10·4	11·0	6·3	with 10
Educational	30·3	28·6	8·9	53·3	54·3	12·0	22·3	20·7	9·4	
Religion	3·0	2·6	4·9	0·4	0·4	5·1	2·0	2·1	5·9	
Campaigning	0·9	1·1	0·1	0·6	0·9	0·0	1·1	0·7	0·3	

N.B. 'Educational' proportions (BBC-2) boosted by Open University broadcasts that can be decided most easily. Once the message has been defined to this extent the range of possibilities for its thematic classification is reduced; the ease with which an analysis of TV content on this two-stage basis may be conducted is evident from the virtually total agreement between judges that we have reported. By isolating the separate dimensions of function and theme in this way we have been able to minimise the interactions between most of the programme genres traditionally used. In discussing certain programme types, however, we have come increasingly to observe relations between the intended function of TV content and the stylistic techniques used in communicating it. The children's programme *Sesame Street*, for example, is basically intended as informative, yet uses entertainment techniques in the process. Its classification by function and theme alone as 'an educational programme' is thus a less than total way of describing it. The combined functional headings particularly ('I as E', 'E = I', 'E as I') exemplify the obvious shortcomings of an analysis based on function and theme alone. On the present rationale, a programme such as *Sesame Street* may logically belong to the informative or 'information as entertainment' categories equally. Clearly many programmes may slide in and out of specific functional classes in this way, wreaking havoc with the analysis generally, if the role of mediating technique in the dynamics of TV content is not now recognised. At the more specific levels of audience research the distinction between the theme and technique of a programme is thus critical, helping to clarify the confusions in the basic taxonomic approach to TV content quite substantially. The presentation of information 'as entertainment' becomes explicable as the communication of thematic material 'using entertainment techniques', and 'E as I' presentation (as in sports news) similarly implies the stylistic use of informative technology. In the next section we shall examine the question of TV presentation in more detail, the producer's use of the techniques at his disposal and the conventional criteria that constrain him.

The criterion of visual interest

The need to examine the TV message's technical characteristics in isolation is clearly evinced by the fact that certain conventional content classifications (e.g. drama, movies, documentary film) refer to questions of technique specifically and cannot be examined analytically on a functional basis at all. Since they achieve a fundamental generic status of their own when media content is broadly described, it is interesting that the mediating techniques themselves should have been so completely overlooked in studies of television's sociological and psychological effects. Drama, for example, treating a diversity of themes, relates to a body of technical principles which, though subject to dynamic modification over time, are at any moment definable. Movies similarly comprise a genre with no thematic identity, but with recognisable characteristics arising from their traditional origin in the cinema. The documentary genre embodies a collection of filmic and narrative techniques with, again, a well-defined tradition. Why then has previous media research pursued the likely effects of thematic content so exclusively? The answer is doubtless that the thematic elements in media content and the functions to which they relate are, as we have seen, relatively stable. The factors relating to mediating technique are, however, far more variable.

As we saw in chapter 1, an essential ingredient of artistry is its 'opaqueness', the degree to which, being novel to the perceiver, its full meaning eludes him and requires consideration. The highest levels of pleasure are those experienced when, through active contemplation, new meanings and values are realised; but at a lower, less intellectual level, satisfaction may also be derived from the novelty value of a stimulus alone (Berlyne, 1960). In animal behaviour, for example, a profuse range of signalling and display rituals has been identified, notably in courtship and threat behaviour; these, as Cook (1975) observes, may broadly be classified in terms of those techniques which attract attention and simultaneously convey a message, and those which simply attract attention, either prior to the transmission of a message or merely to sustain the channel for its own sake. In anthropological contexts such techniques naturally become more sophisticated, prompting further sub-divisions. Tavolga (1970) distinguishes between symbolic and linguistic forms of communication; while the science of linguistics in its own right has generated sub-sub-divisions between, for example, the 'phatic' processes of language (Malinowski, 1953) by which attention is captured, and the 'metalingual' by which mutual understanding is checked and sustained (Jakobson, 1960).

In the broadcasting context, numerous techniques have been developed for the 'phatic' function in particular. The simplest use of a medium's imagery is of course to elicit the lowest level of cognitive response – an interest in its simple novelty value. The criterion of 'visual interest' has dominated TV production since its inception, and is applied in a surprising variety of programme contexts – including, as we have seen, the news (chapter 1). Regardless of programme function or theme, it seems, a TV producer's basic instinct in his effort to produce 'good' (eye-catching, appealing) television is to keep the visual interest of the image sustained at all times. Thus producers in general have become skilled in using between two and four cameras simultaneously to transmit the basic programme content. In a studio current affairs programme one of the cameras will almost certainly be positioned to give a full face close-up of the main presenter (the 'talking head' shot), while the others will be deployed to show different participants − interviewer and interviewee, for example, in alternating sequence, long shots, close-ups and side views, separately, both together, and so on. As the cameras have total flexibility to 'track' and 'pan' up and down and from side to side, so their visual scope is also extended by the use of the magnifying 'zoom lens', which enables continual image variation (in terms of focal length) even when one camera alone is used. Even in the presentation of TV news, it has become common for two presenters to be employed and the news items shared alternately between them (chapter 1). This model was established in the States, emulated first by one channel in Britain and then by the other, and is now a well-established news format. Even before this practice was adopted, however, variations in camera angle were employed to give alternate shots of the presenter, first facing one camera and then the other as he turned (literally) from one news desk to the next. Whilst the origin of this technique may have at least one taproot in 'insurance', since in the early days a stand-by camera was always at hand in case the main one failed, its modern use is justified on the grounds of interest, variety, change of pace from one item to the next, and simple visual expediency.

In practice, however, there are still many other techniques for the producer to use, not all of which are appropriate to news broadcasting but which one would be loath to predict will never become so. In the main these have developed for artistic rather than for functional effects and apace with the medium's increasing electronic sophistication − indeed, they have usually been devised by engineers *before* actual production needs for them have become apparent − and they are used in numerous production contexts 'because they are there'. They include the 'special effects' − the 'wipes' and 'fades', for example, varying from the gradual loss of focus through a waving picture (often used to indicate flashbacks or vague memories surfacing in a TV character's mind) to the split-screen effects created by a combination of images from several camera sources at once: the latter effects are rather similar to drawing a curtain (vertical wipe) or to pulling down a blind (horizontal wipe). Other variations in this category will be familiar to regular viewers of such light entertainment programmes as *Top of the Pops*, in which an elaborate range of multiple images, 'Venetian blind' effects and visual illusion is presented: the use of such techniques occasionally permits the producer to enhance his programme content by reinforcing its meaning in visual terms: thus songs dealing with drugs or 'peak' experiences may be accompanied by pictures placing particular emphasis on certain colours which are reported as being perceived under hallucinogenic influences.

A further development used increasingly to heighten and vary the visual interest of a programme is the technique of 'keying' or 'colour separation overlay', by which the elements of several cameras may be electronically fused. This effect may be used to give the false impression that a performer is actually in front of a relevant background (for example, the Houses of Parliament as the context for a political report). In drama and light entertainment usage, it has equally speedily become a standard means of visual illusion and stylised effect.

Just as some of these techniques have evolved from the sheer technical ability to perform them, so too there are production techniques that are used for combined reasons of visual interest and technical restriction. Editing procedures, for example, enabling the integration and modification of pre-recorded programme material before transmission, are used for numerous planned effects. Ostensibly these are often due to a lack of adequate production resources (as in the example to follow) but they are used for general stylish effects also. When a film unit sets out to record a news interview on location, for instance, typically only one camera is taken in the interests of economy. When the medium of film is used, even simultaneously recorded versions of a scene require after the event integration by a film editor, as only large scale TV control facilities permit spontaneous cutting between cameras; and the possibilities for manipulation of the image and its meaning at the editing stage are well-known. In the one-camera recording of a conversation, the major problem is that only one participant may conveniently be seen at a time and the alternating exchange between both participants is usually unpredictable. For the sake of visual interest and the abbreviation of the recorded material combined, the film editor demands a selection of shots from which he may create an illusion of sequence reflecting that normally possible when more than one camera is available. An acceptable sequence is one in which the edited manipulation of the film is not apparent: thus the image should not give a sudden jump, nor should the performer's expression change unaccountably, nor a particular gesture awkwardly cease. In the location interview, therefore, the camera is normally trained on the respondent for the duration of the interview, after which the interviewer is filmed repeating his questions (in so far as he can remember them) so that the editor may later re-sequence the shots appropriately. At the same time, the opportunity is usually taken to record some general shots of the interviewer acting out 'agreement' and studied interest as appropriate. Shots of this type – referred to as 'cutaways' and 'noddies' respectively – may then be used by the editor to cover over awkward edited joins. Instead of allowing an incongruous hiatus in the picture of an interviewee, he may splice in a shot of the interviewer nodding and then cut back to the interviewee, his expression now changed but not sharply or oddly.

In practice, however, hasty editing under pressure of deadlines may lead to the very effects of jump-cut and hiatus that the process is designed to minimise: to the viewer unaware of the technique used, the frequently inappropriate insertion of a nod or a smirk on the interviewer's part may not actually be recognised as an artefact of the editing but may certainly bewilder. (In unscrupulous hands such effects could of course be created deliberately to make a person appear to avoid a question, to give a silly answer – or even to misrepresent his position by placing his replies in a totally new sequence and context.) The justification for using location material in news and current affairs contexts at all is actually often arguable in its own right. The need felt by news reporters, schooled in journalistic traditions, to report 'from the actual scene' is much in evidence even when there is nothing at the actual scene to remark about or to distinguish it from any other location. From the visual interest point of view a report from outside the building where talks are actually taking place is evidently much more desirable than the same report from inside the studio; and background detail of an airfield where (often fifteen minutes earlier) an aeroplane was hijacked lends a ring of conviction to the most impoverished of verbal accounts: it is 'merely corroborative detail, intended to give artistic verisimilitude to an otherwise bald and unconvincing narrative' (Gilbert, 1884). Where the 'corroborative detail' is not available (as in a telephoned account from overseas) the reporter's photograph is nonetheless similarly superimposed on a picture of the report's place of origin.

All of the techniques we have described exemplify the basic instinct within TV production to 'package' and promote programme content by adding to them the spice of variety which it is assumed the viewer's attention requires. Yet, as we shall demonstrate in the chapters to follow, the use of such techniques may occasionally have quite unexpected side effects (viz. the bewilderment of viewers at the strange effects of hasty editing described above). Easy acceptance of their use is a natural anaesthetic to consideration of the powerful influence they may unintentionally exert over the viewer. As we have indicated, conventional media research has completely overlooked the effects of presentation

34

technique and concentrated instead on the intended content of the performer's message. However, as chapters 3 and 4 indicate, the influences of a performer's own perceived image may actually be primary in the perception of his message content. If his evident function is as an entertainer, he must clearly be seen to have the confident, entertaining air appropriate to such a function; if he is a newsreader, he must have a similarly appropriate air of authority, alertness and reliability. Whatever his function, he must be seen to be credible as a performer in that context; for his message will be viewed in terms of the basic credibility label whenever its sense is ambiguous. (In fact, the emphasis of previous researchers on media subject matter alone may be even further from the mark than we are here implying. A BBC-TV cameraman, when asked by one of the authors to 'zoom in' on a given cue to actually 'magnify' a particular point, was visibly gratified. 'This is great!' he said, 'Usually I never listen to what the people I film are saying, but this way I'm really part of it!'.) Preoccupied by questions of its visual interest alone, those who design the imagery of television may indeed have little occasion to examine finer points of content at all. It is perhaps a surprising possibility, but most important to consider. For how, when they have a particular and meaningful message to impart, do TV mediators actually apply their techniques to the task? Is visual interest actually the sole criterion by which their use of the medium is governed? Or can more effective criteria be applied? Each of these questions is answered in greater depth later in the book (chapters 5 to 7). But in preparation we must recognise that the issues of stylistic strategy that such questions raise are profoundly complicated by their dynamic variability between individuals and over time. And, accordingly, it is useful to see how previous attempts to establish rules for the stylistic analysis of the TV message have fared.

Stylistics and structure

Previous analyses of mediated form have fallen into two distinct schools. The most exhaustive studies — not surprisingly, given the specialist expertise underlying them — have been by the professional mediators (e.g. Bretz, 1962; Davis, 1975) with the intention of providing guidelines in media production. Neads (1976) provides a summary in this tradition of the basic principles involved in contemporary television camerawork and direction. As he indicates, a definition of the stylistic rules of media presentation is in one sense impossible, for in any medium the most creative work is that which breaks conventional ground for the purpose of a novel aesthetic effect: certain criteria are useful, however, in production training. In contrast to this applied style of formal analysis, an academic tradition has developed, primarily from within the schools of literary analysis and linguistics. In literary criticism the definition of stylistic rules is of course a fundamental goal. With the evolution of the visual media — photography, film, television — it was natural that students of the literary media should wish to apply their skills in semantic and syntactic analysis to media in general; and the distinction between the thematic and formal aspects of media communication has thus been accorded a more central role in their tradition than in the general analytic approaches examined previously.

Metz (1974a), for example, with special reference to film, describes the message as an intrinsic organisation of four 'substances': the moving photographic image, recorded noise, phonetic sound and music. The basic unit in the visual image is the *shot*, within which the information is provided, either explicitly or by suggestion, as to any action that may occur, and its context in time and space. Further information in each of these respects is conveyed similarly by the manner in which separate shots are structured, the visual 'syntax' of the sequence in which they are arranged. Between separate shots the action they contain, the spatial context in which it occurs, and the passage of time are normally continuous; shots related on these bases (representing, for example, the various participants in a discussion) build up to form a scene, and a break in the continuity of space, time and action indicates the progression from one scene to the next. Scenes in turn combine to form a unified sequence, or in the case of serialised material, an episodic sequence. And at all levels of the visual sequence, the transition between elements may be accomplished either by a short, sharp 'cut' or by the longer, softer 'fade'. In the filmic medium — even though several cameras may be used — each transition between shots is effected by an editing procedure, as we have seen, and the continuity of space, time and action may equally be quite illusory. In both film and television all three dimensions are manipulated for numerous modish effects by the structural features that may be imposed on the display in this fashion. The rules underlying the stylistic use of visual media may thus indeed be sought in terms of its 'phonological' (formal) and 'syntactic' (sequential) bases in a linguistic manner. In his 'grande syntagmatique' this has been Metz' (1974b) essential purpose.

But as the previous section indicates, the unit on which Metz' syntactical rules are based, the shot, is in itself a quite inadequate reflection of the range of forms mediated material may take. As Inglis

(1975) points out, the films of Miklos Jancso contain ten-minute choreographed, separate shots that defeat traditional stylistic analysis entirely. Within the normally far shorter shot, a universe of imagery similarly remains for definition, and, in basing his syntactic analysis on this relatively gross unit of form, Metz is obliged to look to other sources of meaning for support in his final analysis of the message content. The critical data concerning space, time and action on which Metzian analyses are based thus derive from the syntactic arrangement of the message in part only: the information confirming, even underlying, pure structural analysis lies — as in all other studies of the message that we have examined — in the thematic content and its intended function. To do him full justice, Metz fully acknowledges the inadequacy of his analytic approach in this respect; and in the terms of his approach fully stated (1974b), the interaction of audio-visual syntax and the narrative stylistics of a message are explicitly recognised. In fact, Metz' approach, in treating the visual imagery as a significant system in its own right, gives more insight into the possible nature of the mediated message than do various other prominent theories. That of Vladimir Propp (1958), recently applied to the analysis of the TV message by Silverstone (1975), is a case in point.

Proppian analysis was developed originally in a study of the Russian folktale; it recognises no dependent relationship between the thematic and formal elements of a language, and seeks the underlying rules of the message — as in our broad analyses of schedule allocations earlier in the chapter — in terms of its functional—thematic content alone: technique plays no part. The thirty-one message types Propp identifies (e.g. perpetration of villainy, departure of hero from home, junction of hero and villain in combat), although deriving from the Russian source exclusively, are held to form the basis for human narrative as a whole. In this respect, Propp's approach to linguistic analysis anticipates that of Chomsky (1965), in maintaining the existence of a 'universal' grammar from which all others have evolved; it echoes the doctrines of Jung (1940) on the archetypal concepts operating within the 'collective unconscious'; and it evokes more distant echoes of the theory of universal forms proposed by Plato. It lacks, however, Plato's realism (chapter 1); and it duplicates, unfortunately, the perennial scientific tendency to itemise/ channel/compartmentalise/factorise the phenomenal world by the use of artificial labels, thereby restricting the view for subsequent generations. In conventional psychology, the labelling tendency has accelerated since the development in the late 1920s of factor analytic techniques. The non-empirical approaches favoured by students of language, however, remained free from this tendency until the development of structuralism under the anthropological influence, retaining a sensitivity to the dynamic properties of human communication and the need for fluidity in its measurement. In summary form, the disadvantages of structuralism in the analysis of media dynamics are as follows:

(1)   *Its frequent inability to define the syntactic rules of the medium on a unified phonological rationale.* Any content analysis based on the taxonomic, labelling approach is bound to run into this problem, for either the list of basic elements is too crudely drawn to have descriptive value (as in the visual 'phonological' classification of mediated form by Metz), or it is too complex to be predictive. As the set of syntactic or phonological components in an analytic system proliferates, the possible interactions between them multiply likewise, to the detriment of the system's semantic value. As indicated by Silverstone (1975), for example, not one of the thirty-one narrative elements defined by Propp excludes another; and their actual effects, intended or otherwise, are thus inevitably confounded.

(2)   *Its consequent reliance on a set of universal absolutes whose existence can neither be proved nor denied.* As Lyons (1970) indicates:

> the current concern with 'deeper' and more 'abstract' syntax on the part of many theoreticians makes it all the more important to examine as wide a range of languages as possible. Much of the work so far published which purports to demonstrate the 'universality' of certain 'deeper' analyses of English makes only the most cursory reference to the structure of other languages. (p.139.)

(3)   *Its hypothetical basis on psychological phenomena for which there is no evidence.* The genetic transmission of structural awareness is, again, a notion with no foreseeable hope of being proved; and the analysis of human perceptual phenomena (chapter 3) provides little support for many of the assumptions on which the psycholinguistic rules of syntax are based. Perceptions of neither space, time nor action are in any way the rational, linear processes that traditional structuralist theory relies on; and the human sensitivity to 'deep structure' assumed in Chomskyan theory is, in psychological terms, quite unfounded. Similarly, in Propp's narrative model:

> Apart from the (linear) necessity of one function following another ... there is little reference either to the dynamics at work in the narrative generally, or to the problems associated with the transcendence of chronology in the movement of information. This relative inadequacy is magnified in contemporary narratives, especial-

ly in those presented on film or television. (Silverstone, 1975, p.16.)

Moreover, any analysis of media content according to the structural linguistic approach is bound naturally to favour the dominance of verbal content over visual; the typical structural approach to the visual media is predominantly a treatment of its aural content only. Modern perceptual theory, on the other hand, indicates no such universal dominance between the separate senses (cf. Davidoff, 1975).

(4) *Its ultimate denial of social and cultural factors in the communication process.* As indicated earlier in the discussion of theme and intended function, even the most basic elements of media content are conditioned by the group codes and controls of the ideology to which they belong. And the definition of functional thematic determinants of content in isolation are unable to reflect such factors. Lévi-Strauss (1960) criticises Propp's separation of the narrative and formal aspects of mythology for precisely this reason. By treating the audience as an undifferentiated mass, and its individual members as equally receptive to the codes on which the message is presumed based, the structural approach to message content falls ultimately into the same determinist trap as the conventional approach to media effects in general.

The objections to structuralism are thus equally applied to the 'analysis of the TV message' *per se.* Since theme, intended function, mediated form and audience – each of the central elements we have examined during this chapter – are all ultimately incapable of distinction, it is clear that the dynamic laws relating to media effects can never be determined by analyses of overt content alone. The concretisation of 'the message' is evidently pure artefact; its objective analysis, and attempts at the abstract definition of its stylistic features on simple taxonomic bases, are doomed equally. In Barthes' (1967) view, language and style, though incapable of separation, are individually conditioned anyway. While language is determined by the exterior, cultural factors referred to by Lévi-Strauss, style refers to those internal, personal factors within the writer's history which are as idiosyncratic – and as unintended – as his fingerprints:

> When the writer's choice is to efface both himself and all signs of writing, to aim for a 'zero degree' of writing so that the truth may manifest itself as through a clear pane of glass, what happens according to Barthes is not that he succeeds – the zero degree is as impossible here as in low temperature physics – but that devices must be used to achieve this transparency which are themselves part of the 'speech' ... of his society. (Jamieson, Thompson and

39

Baggaley, 1976, p.21.)

The attempt to efface conventional stylistics and to create an apparent 'zero degree' of TV technique occurs, for example, in the 'drama documentary' in which a new style of realism, or 'television vérité' has been attempted. In British television the form evolved during the late 1960s, and is in effect a modern form of skilled art forgery. To the connoisseur, however, the strategies in use are clearly evident:

> *Leeds United* last week was a posthumous attempt to make a classic 'Wednesday Play' . . . The black-and-white print, and the epic 'Battleship Potemkin' style of filming, made it look like a documentary dug up from the BBC film archives . . . But it drifted into a familiar, spurious form of television realism. There was an interview with the 'Northern Secretary' of a fictitious trade union (identified by a caption across the screen), who talked past the camera in authentic News fashion. A cutter talked about his job straight to camera. Perversely, these tricks did not make the play more 'real'. Instead they served to remind one of the smell of cooking. They announced that here were two actors who were trying to look like trade unionists and cutters appearing on television, and that [the director] was an adept copy-cat when it came to faking the techniques used by his colleagues in Current Affairs. (J. Raban, *Radio Times*, 7 November 1974.)

It is one of the most powerful sources of dynamic change in a creative medium generally that the moment the audience is capable of interpreting the stylistic intentions underlying a programme, the producer must move on to devise new strategies to keep them guessing a while longer.

But despite the constant state of flux in the television art, attempts to decipher the stylistics of the medium using the static techniques of descriptive and structural linguistics are under way. In his sample analyses of a TV sequence by three leading linguistic techniques, Silverstone (1975) acknowledges many cogent objections to their validity in media analysis. Following his identification of twenty-three segments in the sequence — a fifty-two minute drama episode — by Metzian analysis, he concludes that, in terms of its producer's intentions at least, the description of the piece 'feels intuitively correct'. Intuitively, of course, the producer's intentions may never be crystal clear even to himself, and in the handling of a broadcast message so many agents are involved (cf. Enzensberger, 1970; Elliott, 1972; Barr, 1975) that the precise origins and intentionality of the message are obscure in any case: indeed, the very concept of message source at the broadcast level is ultimately as problematic as the concept of its destination, the audience, discussed earlier.

An application of descriptive analysis — in the study of human interaction styles by Flanders (1960) — exemplifies the taxonomic problems described above, where elements overlap so fluidly that their distinction has little meaning. The total disregard shown by Flanders' system for the communicative role of non-verbal behaviour is also a serious shortcoming. In the separate analysis of non-verbal communication specifically, as represented for example by 'proxemics', the study of physical distance cues (Hall, 1963), and 'kinesics', the study of bodily motion (Birdwhistell, 1970), the problems are equally prolific (cf. Thompson, Baggaley and Jamieson, 1975). *The Natural History of an Interview*, for example (McQuown et al., 1971), represents at monograph length an exhaustive kinesic analysis of a single ten-minute conversation: the description of one tiny eighteen-second section fills twenty-three pages. A similar analysis by Frank (1973) of American TV coverage of the 1972 presidential campaign defines many dozens of message elements, though it yields no stylistic information regarding TV news material generally:

> Different findings might well have emerged if the news sample had been noncampaign, or if the campaign had been conducted under different political circumstances (e.g., an incumbent liberal Demo-crat). (Frank, 1973, p.74)

Their complexity and extreme specificity reduce the value of such content studies to the exercise level.

A final and more successful structural account of the television message is given by Hood (1975). The item forming the foundation of Hood's visual grammar is the pictorial image, defined as 'iconic'; images are linked syntactically to form sequences, complete programmes, and ultimately an evening's viewing. Of course, the 'image' is far too open-ended a unit to be descriptive in itself; but Hood's analysis differs from all others we have examined in its emphasis not merely on the underlying representational codes and conventions employed by producers, but on their implications as decided by the viewer. 'The fact that [codes] can be read by the receivers', states Hood, 'argues that there is a congruence between the coding and decoding process.' The need to consider the much overlooked decoding process specifically was indicated, with particular reference to

41

the educational media, by Baggaley (1973b), in the observation that students should be versed in the codes of TV presentation before they may decode them for educational gain: and we develop this case in chapter 6. The common ground between the statements of both Hood and Baggaley is the analytical emphasis each places on the interpretation of the message as well as on its intentionality. The act of interpretation enters into all perceptual processes, particularly when a wide range of observations must be squeezed into a narrow range of cognitive structures. The need of Proppian analysts, for example, to identify the elements of heroism and villainy in a piece causes considerable problems in interpreting contemporary narrative form, where anti-heroism flourishes and dramatic conflict may derive from the tensions of the situation. Silverstone's (1975) interpretation of a character's heart attack as the villain in a contemporary TV series, *Intimate Strangers*, is a good example of the distortion arising from over-zealous classification in this way. (The very softening of black and white shades in contemporary TV fiction was discussed by Tinker, 1975.) The analysis of message effects clearly cannot depend on such *a priori* criteria alone. And since, throughout this chapter, every one of the areas of intentionality we have referred to (intended function, intended audience, intended effect, etc.) has necessarily been defined in terms of one or more person's *interpretations* of it, we must clearly proceed to an analysis of the intention and interpretation dichotomy specifically.

Intention and interpretation

The distinction between intention and interpretation in the analysis of the message forms a central pivot in our argument. Intention may be defined by interpretation alone: the definition of intended features of a message is an interpretation in itself. In conventional communication terminology (chapter 1) the dichotomy goes unheeded. It is agreed that a message is conveyed through an information channel to its receiver, and that a responding message may be elicited, thereby completing the circuit; but as Rowntree (1975) indicates, two-way 'communication' only occurs when the one-way 'municative' message has been interpreted successfully. The basic Shannon and Weaver (1949) model, representing human communication in engineering terms, allows for failures in the circuit by the confusion of the message (signal) with 'noise' factors. But the source of the confusion is still ambiguous, as the model makes no allowance for the types of failure for which the sender, the receiver, and the channel itself

42

may be separately responsible.

The problem of matching the sender's intention and the receiver's interpretation of that intention in successful communication is indicated by Mackay (1969):

> ... with a different pattern of past experience or a different set of goal priorities, it is possible for one human organism to have evolved a single complex organiser to represent a feature of the world almost (if not quite) beyond the conceptual group of another, whose organising system could cope with it only at the cost of major dismantling and rebuilding operations. Since the same is likely to be true in reverse, we have here a most potent and subtle source of failure of human communication. (p.113)

He later qualifies this analysis, slightly elaborately, in terms of 'goal-directedness' (Mackay, 1972):

> Signalling is widely used as a neutral word for the activity of transmitting information, regardless of whether or not the activity is goal-directed, and what impact, if any, it has on the recipient ... Its use would allow us to say, for example, that 'A is signalling, but not communicating' in circumstances where information is being transmitted from A but not affecting the organising system of any recipient ... (p.6)

The relationship between the 'goal-direction' of a message and its interpretations are illustrated in Fig. 2.5; whether or not a message has an (intended) goal at all, its impact (on interpretation) is unknown.

In discussing, formulating and organising his ideas in this characteristic way, Mackay is of course indebted almost entirely to the cybernetic, information flow model of communication. In this respect, Mackay and another cybernetician may be described as sharing the same 'organising system', as having developed 'a single complex organiser to represent a feature of the world' presumably within the other's grasp. But if others do not interpret their views as easily, it is possible that the 'organising system'

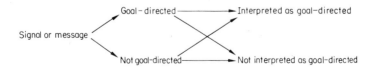

Fig. 2.5 Interpretation and goal-direction (reprinted from Jamieson, Thompson and Baggaley, 1976, p.21)

43

is itself too complex and overladen for the meaning it represents. The potential for communication failure that Mackay's analysis describes may certainly be represented with relative simplicity. Compare, for instance, the traditional model of the communication circuit (chapter 1) with the expression given in Fig. 2.6(a) below.

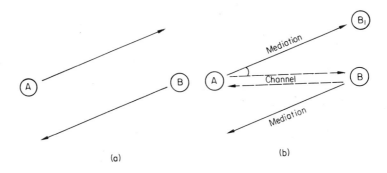

(a)   (b)

Fig. 2.6   Communication as fallible process (mediation vs. channel)

The actual implications of Fig. 2.6(a) and the conventional circuit model are the same: for each fairly describes situations in which a message is emitted from source A and a subsequent message emitted from A's destination, source B. Like all other determinist models they express intention to communicate and *assume* an effect. Only Fig. 2.6(a), however, recognises that, in the exchange of messages involving human agency at least, communication may fail. In the traditional model, concepts such as message, medium and channel are quite undifferentiated; and even with the addition of a 'noise' component as in Shannon and Weaver's (1949) model, there is nothing to express the extent to which source A's message is successfully received, and the relationship of message B to it. In the present context, however, the message, its channel and the mediating technology that conveys it have each been regarded as entirely separate expressions; and on this basis the possibilities of both success and failure in attempted communication may be represented jointly, as in Fig. 2.6(b). The only circular component in this figure is described by the dotted lines, a representation of channel (the *intention* to communicate *shared by A and B equally*). A total match between the intentional and the interpreted characteristics of the message occurs in the ideal channel only, which is an abstraction. At source, and in terms of the effect for which it is intended, a message may be quite explicit, but if

44

mediated inadequately its purpose is thwarted: whatever the message's intentional characteristics, its progress and fate is thus viewed in terms of its mediated form, as represented by the bold lines. The degree to which a message, for various reasons, may fail to strike home at its destination B is described by the angle BAB_1 and the probability that message B follows message A as the actual and appropriate outcome of it is a function of A's accurate mediation and interpretation combined.

An analogy to this model is the situation in which invaders scale the ramparts of a fortress. If the distance (or channel) between the ground and battlements appears viable, the intention to span it is formed. A ladder is erected as the medium by which the effort is to be made, and one human message after another prepares to storm it. Some may abandon the attempt before leaving the ground, deciding that the channel is after all insurmountable; others may fall off the ladder, lacking the strength or technique to climb it. The ladder itself may prove inadequate — either too weak for the weight conveyed, or too short for the wall — and even if a message reaches the top, where the defenders may be either inhospitable or dead, as in *Beau Geste*, it still has to cope with the problem of its reception. In the whole process, the ladder and its use, and the type of reception that the message encounters, are the central determinants of the outcome. In the study of communication effects generally, the analysis of mediated form and its interpretations are similarly basic; the traditional inspection of media content is useful for superficial analytical purposes only, since the relationships between components are indistinct and certain terminology is seriously confused. 'The medium' and 'the message', for example: these are both profoundly related, as McLuhan (1967) realised. But the conventional determinist approach he espouses is a study of channel, the theoretical abstract expressing *intended* characteristics of the message only. The medium — i.e. mediating technology, be it television, the theatre, or a language — is a separate question entirely. And McLuhan's 'the medium *is* the message' thus expresses, by dramatic elision, a confusion between medium and channel functions that communication theorists must henceforward resolve.

The emphasis on interpretation in this argument returns us directly to Kelly's (1955) personal construct theory, which was mentioned in chapter 1. As far as Kelly is concerned, man is an inquirer: he regulates his life and his behaviour by forming hypotheses about the world and what will happen, and by noting the criteria that most assist him in the hypothetic–deductive process. The individual's use of these criteria, or 'constructs', becomes habitual: they are entirely of his own devising and

45

are thus personal to him — though, whether through laziness or unoriginality or sheer convenience, it usually turns out that individuals share a certain proportion of their constructs with others in their culture (Duck, 1973). Owing to the individual's unique constructive potential, however, neither his own reactions, nor the extent of their similarity to those of others, is ever entirely predictable. In the present context, this means that the reactions expected by a producer or researcher may not actually be those manifested by the viewer at all, who with his different personality and experience perceives the television display (visually and aurally) on entirely different bases. His information selection is possibly different; his assessment of the information is possibly different; his reaction to it is different again. (We say 'possibly' to underline the fact that this notion, although important, has been woefully under-researched.) However, Kelly states that:

> While the constructs are personal and each individual has his own repertory of them, they are not so inaccessibly private that we human beings must despair of ever understanding each other.

And in the 'role construct repertory test' (Reptest), Kelly provides an ingenious tool for analysing an individual's interpretation of phenomena without needing recourse to

> ... single-dimensional behavioural formulas, to physiological terms, to historical determinisms, to autonomous motives, or to any of the other reductionistic schemes that psychologists commonly employ. The psychology of personal constructs is then essentially a methodological psychology rather than the usual content psychology, though, of course, it yields content as a secondary product.

Though the orthodox use of personal construct methodology is in the study of people's perceptions of each other (Duck, 1973), it is applicable in the assessment of individual interpretations whatever the subject matter. As a tool on which our initial hypotheses in media research may be based, the value of the Reptest has been indicated by Baggaley (1973b): it is

> in effect 'a questionnaire without questions', [permitting] us to draw from the audience the information we require without biasing them towards our own construction of the situation. (p.165)

In order to demonstrate the different constructions that may be placed upon media materials, the following experiment was conducted. A sequence of five educational extracts, each between two and five minutes long was presented to three groups of subjects: TV production trainees, teachers familiar with the use of TV in the classroom, and a neutral group of undergraduate students. Each subject was then asked to recall and compare the extracts according to the Reptest formula. The test indicates the aspects of the material to which subjects have individually been sensitive; and on this occasion these variables were classified as either relating to its thematic content (whether or not extracts referred to scientific principles, for example) or to its mediated form (e.g. whether or not graphics were used). The proportion of responses related to thematic and formal aspects of the presentation in the three subject groups is given here in Fig. 2.7.

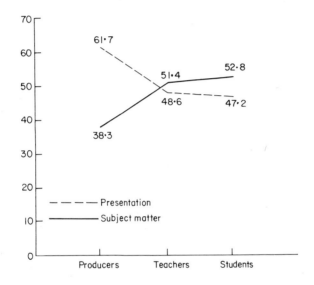

Fig. 2.7   Group differences in responses to TV material

Differences between the groups as to their relative interest in thematic and formal elements in the TV message are clearly indicated. Both the teachers (Group 2) and the neutral students (Group 3) give approximately equal weighting to both types of element, though the trainee producers (Group 1) demonstrate, by comparison, an over-emphasised attention to the formal elements: the suspicion that producers may actually concentrate on presentation criteria in their design of TV material at the expense of the thematic exposition will be recalled from earlier in the

47

chapter.

As Kelly himself recognises (1955), the constructs elicited by the Reptest are not necessarily the only constructs operating in the individual's personal construction system; many others incapable of immediate verbal expression may also exert an influence on his personal view of the world. The value of a personal construct approach in the present context, however, is particularly apparent, indicating the immense diffusion of effects that media material may exert, which, combined with the difficulties of defining its causes, renders the definitive analysis of TV message content *per se* quite impossible. By examining the factors underlying the perception and interpretation of TV material in such ways, we become able to define the dynamic properties of television and the viewing experience inferentially. Indeed, in any attempt to identify the effects of a medium, it is more logical for us to begin in this way, as close as possible to their psychological basis, than it is to proceed in isolation from them as by previous methods. To ignore the viewer in TV research, and to assume that one is much like any other, is clearly to ignore the problem.

Summary

(1)   Traditional analyses of television's effects are based on definitions of its content alone. Audience appreciation data, for instance, are analysed in terms of *ad hoc* programme groupings in which thematic, functional and technical characteristics of the message are confounded.

(2)   For practical analytical purposes, the most stable relationship between message characteristics occurs between the informative or entertainment function of a TV message and its thematic content. The identity of function and theme provides a basis for certain restricted analyses of the message within a given ideology.

(3)   On a functional–thematic basis, aspects of TV programme scheduling may be examined. The thematic balance in TV output within and between separate broadcasting organisations may be compared, for example, within the weekly cycle and over time.

(4)   A criterion by which TV production is predominantly governed is that of visual interest. However, techniques used for the sole purpose of arousing and sustaining viewers' attention to programme content may also have unwitting side-effects on its apparent credibility.

(5)   Stylistic analyses of TV technique and form are possible by descriptive and structural linguistic techniques, though these ultimately

48

suffer from the same theoretical and interpretative problems as conventional content analyses.

(6) A depth study of the television medium is made possible by the distinction between its intended effects and their interpretation. Traditional analyses (of media processes via content) reflect intended characteristics alone, whereas the reverse approach (i.e. to content via interpretation) permits insight into television's psychological properties.

References

Baggaley, J. P. (1973b), 'Developing an effective educational medium', *Programmed Learning and Educational Technology*, vol. 10.

Barr, C. (1975), 'Upstairs, downstairs', paper read to the Conference of the Society for Education in Film and Television, Birkbeck College, London.

Barthes, R. (1967), *Writing Degree Zero*, London, Cape.

Bateson, G. (1973), *Steps to an Ecology of Mind*, St Albans, Herts., Paladin.

Berlyne, D. E. (1960), *Conflict, Arousal and Curiosity*, New York, McGraw-Hill.

Birdwhistell, R. L. (1970), *Kinesics and Context*, Philadelphia, University of Pennsylvania Press.

Bretz, R. (1962), *Techniques of Television Production*, London, McGraw-Hill.

Burke, K. (1945), *A Grammar of Motives*, New Jersey, Prentice-Hall.

Chomsky, N. (1965), *Aspects of the Theory of Syntax*, Cambridge, Mass., MIT Press.

Cook, R. (1975), 'Communication and learning: an ethological approach', in Baggaley, J. P., Jamieson, G. H. and Marchant, H. (eds), *Aspects of Educational Technology VIII*, Bath, Pitman Press.

Dannheisser, P. (1975), 'A closer look at the audience', *Independent Broadcasting*, 3.

Davidoff, J. B. (1975), *Differences in Visual Perception*, London, Crosby Lockwood Staples.

Davis, D. (1975), *The Grammar of Television Production*, revised by Wooler, M., London, Barrie and Jenkins.

Duck, S. W. (1973), *Personal Relationships and Personal Constructs: A Study of Friendship Formation*, London, Wiley.

Elliott, P. (1972), *The Making of a Television Series*, London, Constable.

Enzensberger, H. M. (1970), 'Constituents of a theory of the media', *New Left Review,* 64.

Flanders, N. A. (1960), 'Interaction analysis in the classroom: a manual for observers', reprinted in Amidon, E. J. and Hough, J. B. (eds) *Interaction Analysis: Theory, Research and Application,* London, Addison Wesley.

Frank, R. S. (1973), *Message Dimensions of Television News,* Lexington, Mass., D. C. Heath.

Gilbert, W. S., 'The Mikado', reprinted in *The Savoy Operas,* vol. 2, London, Oxford University Press, 1963.

Goodhardt, G. J., Ehrenberg, A. S. C. and Collins, M. A. (1975), *The Television Audience: Patterns of Viewing,* Farnborough, Saxon House.

Hall, E. T. (1963), 'A system for the notation of proxemic behavior', *Amer. Anthropol.,* vol. 65.

Hood, S. (1975), 'Visual literacy examined', in Luckham, B. (ed.), *Proceedings of the Sixth Symposium on Broadcasting Policy – 'Audio-Visual Literacy',* University of Manchester.

Howitt, D. and Cumberbatch, G. (1976), 'Media research and ETV policy', *Journal of Educational Television,* vol. 2, no. 2.

Inglis, R. (1975), 'Studying teledrama', paper read to the Conference of the Society for Education in Film and Television, Birkbeck College, London.

Jakobson, R. (1960), 'Linguistics and poetics', in Sebeok, T. A. (ed.), *Style in Language,* Cambridge, Mass., MIT Press.

Jamieson, G. H., Thompson, J. O. and Baggaley, J. P. (1976), 'Intention and interpretation in the study of communication', *Journal of Educational Television,* vol. 2, no. 1.

Jung, C. G. (1940), *Archetypes of the Collective Unconscious,* vol. 9, London, Routledge and Kegan Paul.

Kelly, G. A. (1955), *The Psychology of Personal Constructs,* New York, Norton.

Lasswell, H. D. (1948), 'The structure and function of communications', in Bryson, L. (ed.), *The Communication of Ideas,* New York, Harper.

Lévi-Strauss, C. (1960), *La structure et la forme. Réflexions sur un ouvrage de Vladimir Propp,* Paris, Cahiers de L'Institut des Sciences Economiques Appliquées.

Lyons, J. (1970) (ed.) *New Horizons in Linguistics,* Harmondsworth, Penguin.

Malinowski, B. (1953), 'The problem of meaning in primitive languages', in Ogden, C. K. and Richards. I. A. (eds), *The Meaning of Meaning,* London, Routledge and Kegan Paul.

Mackay, D. M. (1969), *Information, Mechanism and Meaning,* Cambridge,

Mass., MIT Press.

Mackay, D. M. (1972), 'Formal analysis of communicative processes', in Hinde, R. A. (ed.), *Non-Verbal Communication*, Cambridge, Cambridge University Press.

McLuhan, M. (1967), *The Medium is the Message*, New York, McGraw-Hill.

McQuown, N. E., Bateson, G., Birdwhistell, R. L., Brosen, H. W. and Hockett, C. F. (1971), *The Natural History of an Interview*, Microfilm Collection of Manuscripts in Cultural Anthropology, Chicago, University of Chicago Library.

Metz, C. (1974a), 'Methodological propositions', *Screen*, 14, 1/2.

Metz, C. (1974b), *Film Language: A Semiotics of the Cinema*, New York, Oxford University Press.

Neads, C. (1976), 'TV production − a student guide', *Journal of Educational Television*, vol. 2, no. 1.

Propp, V. (1958), *Morphology of the Folktale*, Publication 10 of the Research Center in Anthropology, Folklore and Linguistics, Indiana University Press.

Rowley, C. (1975), 'ITV's programme balance 1970−75, *Independent Broadcasting*, 6.

Rowntree, D. (1975), 'Two styles of communication and their implications for learning', in Baggaley, J. P., Jamieson, G. H. and Marchant, H. (eds), *Aspects of Educational Technology VIII*, London, Pitman Press.

Shannon, C. E. and Weaver, W. (1949), *The Mathematical Theory of Communication*, Urbana, University of Illinois Press.

Silverstone, R. (1975), 'Structural analysis of the television message', paper read to the Conference of the Society for Education in Film and Television, Birkbeck College, London.

Tavolga, W. N. (1970), 'Levels of interaction in animal communication', in Aronson, L., Toback, E., Lehrman, D. S. and Rosenblatt, J. S. (eds), *Development and Evolution of Behavior,* New York, Freeman.

Thompson, J. O., Baggaley, J. P. and Jamieson, G. H. (1975), 'Representation, review, and the study of communication', *Journal of Educational Television*, vol. 1, no. 1.

Tinker, J. (1975), Review, *Daily Mail*, 12 December.

Williams, R. (1974), *Television: Technology and Cultural Form*, London, Fontana.

Wober, M. (1975), 'Children and television', *Independent Broadcasting*, 2.

3 Analysis of the viewing experience

It is evident from the previous chapter that the viewer is no mere receiver of transmitted information as implied in the engineering model of human communication, but an active processor of it who interprets the world in characteristic ways determined by his background and personality. Accordingly, a theoretical and methodological framework is required in which the effects deriving from viewers' creativity may be examined. Traditional theories of perception suggest that the viewer sees the elements of a stimulus array in patterns — as something more than the sum of its parts. And since our previous analysis has indicated the need to consider the ways in which the individual forms hypotheses about what he sees, it is appropriate that we should now examine the kind of cues to which viewers respond with 'pattern-forming' hypotheses.

The psychological literature in which the relevant evidence in this respect is reported is extensive, and it is thus all the more surprising that it has been totally overlooked in the analysis of the media. In order to draw the fullest attention to this oversight, we review this literature in the present chapter in some detail, and we indicate that, without due attention to its theoretical implications, analyses of the visual media henceforward will certainly be incomplete.

Perceptual organisation

The nature of perception is such that we are frequently called upon to supply information that is not actually there. The retina of the eye, for example, has a blind spot at which the light sensitive cells are interrupted by the optic nerve. Individuals do not, however, see gaps in the environment in ways that reflect the positioning of this blind spot: instead the brain supplies the missing information in ways that are consistent with what the rest of the eye is observing. The role of expectation in perception is thus critical. A baby quickly learns that when an object disappears from sight it has not necessarily been annihilated (cf. Harris, 1975): the two-dimensional image on the retina (or television set) is interpreted in three-dimensional terms through past experience as a whole. Experience in viewing other people teaches us similarly that a face shown in close-up on a cinema screen is not really twenty metres high, but is likely in reality to belong to a person whose head is of quite a normal size. It is evident that a knowledge of the usual physical properties of stimuli is of prime perceptual importance.

But what are the bases on which the physical properties of a stimulus are judged? According to the Gestalt theorists (Koffka, 1935), perception is based on a search for *Prägnanz* (for 'goodness' in objects, inclusiveness, harmony, conciseness, maximum symmetry and similarity, relative simplicity, completeness). Until the brain has grouped the separate elements of a stimulus display in meaningful configurations, seeking for wholes ('Gestalts') even when they may not exist, perception cannot truly be said to have taken place. Thus, perception of the whole precedes perception of the parts; and the latter is dependent on the perception of the whole that is reached. Descriptively at least the Gestaltist notions are most useful. (We may appreciate the search for *Prägnanz* in terms of our ability to ignore the easily visible linear components of the TV image, interpreting it as an uninterrupted whole.) The cognitive search for meaning — stressed by Bartlett (1932) in his studies of memory — underlies a wide range of perceptual theory from the phenomenon of size constancy (above) to the familiar visual illusion figures (Gregory, 1966). In the light of Gestalt theory it does not seem surprising that the study of TV message parts, as in the last chapter, has failed to provide a meaningful insight into the viewing experience as a whole. Considering perception as ordered on the holistic principle in general, it is reasonable to assume TV viewing to be similarly based.

For an idea of the actual dynamic processes underlying perception, however, we must turn to the theoretical approaches of depth psychology and to the various internal/external factors by which perception is organised. The individual may be influenced by internal motivational factors to 'misperceive' his environment in numerous ways. For example, Bruner and Postman (1948) showed that deprived individuals over-estimate the size of coins: similarly Beams (1954) noted that, when hungry and presented with ambiguous visual images, subjects are inclined to believe they are seeing food objects when they are not. The role of internal, emotional factors in perception has been studied in detail by Bruner and Postman (1947a, b), while the effects of all internal factors may be summed up in terms of one word — 'set' (Postman and Egan, 1949):

In its broadcast sense, set denotes a readiness to respond to stimulus objects in a selective way, to respond to some objects and specific characteristics rather than others. By its set, the organism is selectively tuned to events in the environment. (p.327).

The perceptual role of environmental factors has of course been demonstrated in its own right, most dramatically via the sensory deprivation experiments of, for example, Bexton, Heron and Scott (1954), and Heron, Doane and Scott (1956). Individuals confined to a bleak, unstimulating environment tend to develop marked perceptual and cognitive malfunctions; and naturally the more prolonged the exposure to a perceptual condition, the more permanent the perceptual anomaly it produces. On the other hand, the more enriched the environment, the more likely an individual is to benefit from it both perceptually and cognitively. A child reared in a varied, stimulating environment has far more opportunity to develop as an intelligently perceptive adult than one brought up in more bleak surroundings. Studies (e.g. Newman, Freeman and Holzinger, 1937) which compared the effects of different surroundings on identical twins testify to this, lending as much importance to environmental factors in the perceptual learning process as to internal factors, presumed hereditary. The most permanent, unconscious and influential conditioner of perception in this manner is the very social culture in which we live: the importance of cultural and sub-cultural factors is seen at all levels of perception from the most general to the most specific.

We are dwelling upon the wide-ranging influences on perception to this extent since these are the basic factors, in all their solemn complexity, that the determinist approach to media effects is content to overlook. As we have seen, the assumption that an audience's individual members are grossly similar in their perceptual outlook permits the researcher to draw conclusions regarding certain broad questions of media effect, but little may be concluded of a medium's subtle psychological effects as long as such assumptions persist. In the attempt to unify their many observations, psychologists have generally lacked a theory sufficiently comprehensive to rationalise that most complex of phenomena, the personality, subsuming all of the dynamic factors we have discussed: the study of media is one of many areas to have suffered in consequence. In traditional personality theories, the individual is passed in effect through a number of psychological sieves — the tests on which the theory is based — and the most commonly observed features of his personality 'stick to the sides' for subsequent labelling. Thus Gough (1958) classified subjects' answers to some 400 questions and arranged them in categories of scores on femininity, dominance, tolerance, psychological mindedness, and so forth. Similarly, and more influentially, Eysenck and Eysenck (1964) classified individuals in terms of the two personality components, extraversion and neuroticism: for a time Eysenck's dual factors coped adequately with the broad range of behaviour under measurement, until observations forced the addition of a third factor, psychoticism. In this we see a dilemma that scientists face: confronted by the startling complexity of observations that they have undertaken to explain, they need labels for them, a vocabulary to manipulate. But the labels that fit the majority of observable phenomena avert attention from the minority occurrences and from the processes underlying all phenomena. Kelly's personal construct theory, however, as we have hinted before, emphasises not the lumps into which personality may be classified by outsiders, but the processes going on in the individual's head and exemplified in his behaviour. Although predating the factorial approaches cited here, it is now assuming a role of increasing research importance in clinical and other applications (Bannister and Mair, 1968; Duck, 1973). Similarly, it provides a framework within which to analyse media processes.

Message labelling

As the basis of perception is interpretation (see above) so the basis of interpretation, Kelly indicates, is a set of hypotheses formed on observable bases. There are many examples in socio-psychological literature of the extent to which hypotheses based on even the most simple perceptual cues can distort behaviour in the most bizarre ways, and they serve to illustrate that even in apparently passive observers of TV material some far-reaching effects may be created. As evinced in the act of scientific thought itself, it appears that the formation of individual hypotheses is affected by the 'labelling' of information in a certain way, either by an external agent or by the perceiver himself: the label given may affect the interpretation of the information and the perception of its source equally.

In an examination of the ways in which subjects could be induced to form strange hypotheses by simple situational cues, Orne and Scheibe (1964) decorated a room with elaborate paraphernalia, and provided a button marked 'Panic'. Left in this room, subjects swiftly jumped to conclusions as to the fate awaiting them and began to exhibit panicky behaviour due to the environmental cues alone. Farina, Allen and Saul

(1968) used a similar stratagem to determine individuals' reactions to labels applied not simply to a situation but to themselves. Subjects were asked to write out a fake autobiography, describing either an average and uneventful life, inclinations to homosexuality, or a history of mental illness. Each subject's account was then given (so the subjects believed) to an experimental partner, though in fact the actual account handed across was invariably one of the 'average' type. However, the subjects who believed that their partner had formed a strongly negative impression of them from the account subsequently behaved in such a way that their partner eventually formed a negative impression of them in reality. A similar experiment, classic of its type, was conducted by Kelley (1950). He gave written information to a lecture class concerning the new lecturer who was about to speak to them; strategically, however, he presented the two halves of the class with different versions. In fact, only one word in the two accounts differed, leading one half of the class to believe the lecturer was a 'warm' man, and the other that he was 'cold'. This subtle variation profoundly affected the two groups' subsequent assessments of the lecturer's performance and personal credibility — even though they both saw precisely the same lecture at precisely the same time. More recently, Brand (1973) has shown that merely labelling someone 'neurotic' has the effect of inducing subjects to perceive his behaviour as odd. Such experiments as a whole have obvious implications for TV presentation where individual presenters are labelled in various ways, and where political debate is often described in terms such as 'left-wing', 'extremist', and 'moderate'. The immediate possibility is that, although for reasons of impartiality obvious methods of 'cueing' viewers are usually avoided, various subliminal effects may affect the viewers' perception of the television performer and thus their interpretation of what he says. (This hypothesis is one that we shall pursue in detail in chapter 4.)

The earliest investigations of attitude change demonstrated the influence of an audience's faith in a particular source of information in precisely this way. Hovland and Weiss (1952) gave college students four different articles attributed to high or low credibility sources. Individual articles were more often seen as fair, and their conclusions well justified, when they were attributed to sources of high rather than low credibility. The attitude change induced by the high credibility labels was estimated as over three times greater than that caused by the low credibility labels. Clearly, when the function of a TV broadcast is intended to be informative (news/education/persuasion, etc.), cues to credibility are likely to be an extremely influential determinant of its intended effect. They may be derived at various levels of consciousness: from a reporter's overt claim that his information (or, more often, speculation) is from 'a highly reliable source', or from some other cue suggesting the reporter's own authoritativeness *per se*. Indeed, individual viewers may remember the cues indicating authority and reliability long after the content of the message and the influence it exerted is forgotten. In an experiment conducted by Kelman and Hovland (1953) articles were presented to subjects as in the Hovland and Weiss study. An opinion test three weeks later showed that the differences in attitude between the subjects who had read high or low credibility articles had diminished, but when the source of the articles was reaffirmed, the difference reappeared. Though the thematic impact of the message had worn off, that of the source remained.

Of course, the interpretation of messages may not always proceed on such rational bases; the simple visual interest of a display plays a vital role in the transmission and reception of information, as has been indicated in chapter 2. The power of less obvious visual cues to interpretation has been convincingly demonstrated (cf. the discussion of television and persuasion, chapter 5). Thus, Mitchell and Byrne (1973), in a study of courtroom jury judgements, examined the interaction of perceptual cues with personality. They identified a specific characteristic of authoritarian personalities: that such persons are far more likely to declare a defendant 'not guilty' if he or she is physically attractive. On the subject of authoritarianism specifically, Robbins (1975) has investigated the process by which such personalities arrive at hypotheses regarding other people: he found that, when presented with inconsistent information about others, authoritarian subjects were faster in judgement than other personality types, more confident that they were correct, and less willing to change their minds. From each of these examples, it is evident that the actual content of stimulus input (in the sense of words spoken or messages otherwise conveyed) is by no means the only significant influence on the nature of its reception: in any assessment of, for example, accusations of bias or unfairness in a TV report this is a particularly important point to be remembered. It is equally evident that the actual origins of a message's effect are to be found in terms to which its own qualities and those of its source relate equally: the context in which it is perceived.

Content and context

Every basic cue to perception and interpretation is a product of context in one respect or another. Their effects may be either conscious or unconscious, intentional or accidental. Social psychologists normally observe the effects of context on behaviour by a deliberate stratagem making use of deviously calculated prior information. (The prior information afforded by labelling strategies has been examined in the previous section.) DeCharms, Carpenter and Kuperman (1965), however, gave subjects prior information of a more subtle variety: as to whether or not two people liked one another. The two people in question were then observed discussing whether one of them should do something against his will. When the latter eventually agreed, the subjects believing the two to like one another decided that he had changed his mind as the result of a reasoned judgement reached independently; the other group decided that he had been a pawn in the hands of his partner and had been coerced into doing something to which he was still fundamentally opposed.

Numerous workers have demonstrated the equally profound effects of simultaneous context on social perception. Kelley and Woodruff (1956), for example, showed that the composition and behaviour of an audience can influence other hearers (the experimental subjects) in their endorsement of what has been said: the specific results indicated that the persuasiveness of a communication is influenced by the subjects' belief that the second audience approved of it. Landy (1972) has supported and refined this position in an experiment investigating the effect of simultaneous and previous cues combined: his subjects rated a message more positively when they were told that an attractive rather than an unattractive audience was listening, whether or not that audience appeared to approve of it. It appears that when subjects believe that a speaker on television is addressing an attractive (rather than simply an approving) audience, they assess him on his own merits; but if they believe that an unattractive audience is being addressed, then his credibility is somehow undermined and his arguments are seen as more suspect (Duck and Baggaley, 1975a; and chapter 4).

Of course, so many interactions at this level are possible that speculation of this sort can be risky. For yet another contextual factor by which the impact of a stimulus can be modified is that of *contrast*, an important source of perceptual phenomena generally. Levy (1960) demonstrated the effects of context through contrast by placing single photographs of 'neutral' faces among other photographs depicting faces which looked 'tense'. Instead of seeing the neutral portraits as neutral, observers saw them (in the context of the 'tense' photographs) as 'extremely relaxed'. By this and other tests, Levy was able to show that the normal perception of the photographs was capable of being biased by the contrast factor alone (cf. the Eisenstein experiment on juxtaposition of film shots: chapter 1). The collected evidence from such studies is seemingly bewildering in its diversity, but a key perceptual factor to emerge from them all is one of sequence. In the visual media even simultaneous relationships between points in space, time and action are usually represented as discrete sequential segments (chapter 2) and the viewer's ability to interpret them depends entirely on his knowledge of the sequential codes employed. It follows, moreover, from the arguments concerning hypothesis formation in general that information gathered first — as long as it is meaningful — is most influential, setting the scene and suggesting a construction into which later information will fit.

Naturally, the formation of hypotheses is a continual process of modification and reshaping. After hearing an extreme positive attitude to something, subjects regard an extreme negative attitude as less extreme and more moderate than they had rated it initially (Mascaro and Graves, 1973). So the simple sequencing of message elements is yet again only one of the factors that may cause an argument to have more or less of an effect than is actually intended. To achieve a properly balanced TV report, therefore, it matters not merely what is said first, but also how the opposite points are couched (do they constitute replies to earlier points, for example), how the reporter treats each point, and how he concludes. When the viewers are ignorant of the subject matter, the reporter's role in the argument is all the more important, for in such conditions, as Festinger (1954) indicates, the observer is forced to use less rational bases for his judgements — and the need for careful control over the argument becomes crucial. The situation in which the marginal, irrational effects on observer responses are therefore likely to be strongest is one of 'maximum ambiguity' (Scheff, 1973) in which neither the subject matter nor the source are previously known to the observer. Thus Hovland, Lumsdaine and Sheffield (1949) found that the presentation of a one-sided argument was effective enough with poorly educated listeners, though both sides of the argument were required in preaching to the highly educated. (A one-sided argument also tends to convince the listener more easily if it is similar to his existing view.) If the presentation is truly well-balanced then the effects of the two sides tend to cancel out. Actual conversion of opinion is of course more probable if explicit conclusions are drawn than if the receiver is left to draw his own. As Hovland and Mandell (1952) indicate, possibly the best and most neutral way to present an argument is therefore to offer more than one aspect of the case and to draw explicit conclusions from them each; but this very act of drawing explicit conclusions in an argument is precisely that which TV presenters, in the very quest for impartiality, are denied.

Indeed, so many factors are involved in the encoding–decoding process of television that attempts to identify and control the medium's dynamics on the basis of conscious criteria, even those of intention and interpretation combined, are quite impracticable. One of the enjoyable features of parliamentary election campaigns, in fact, is hearing members of each of the political parties complain simultaneously that a given programme was biased against them specifically. While watchdog authorities have been careful to scrutinise the content of programmes, the procedures used and the equity of treatment for some time, the criteria hitherto available to them by which to recognise that an effect has occurred are far too simple for the complex arguments of bias that may occur. For just as the viewer may clearly respond to contextual cues that the producer has featured deliberately, so it is equally conceivable that he is able to ignore the producer's codes and to use in his decoding process cues that are unsuspected by himself and the producer alike. It is in the viewer's natural — even irrepressible — tendency to form hypotheses at this level that the most complex source of television's dynamics lies. And in order to unravel it we must consider the characteristic ways in which television presents its information, the ways in which a TV performer is presented to the audience, both explicitly and implicitly, and the styles of social interaction in which television performers engage. The analysis conducted in the next section is thus germane to TV output serving an informative function in particular (interviews, current affairs programmes, news presentations, etc.). No immediate reference will be made to plays and light entertainment, though the analysis will be seen to refer directly to these in due course. We are particularly concerned for the present with those aspects of television content that deal with 'real life' information, and with the extent to which television methods permit the viewer to gather this information as he would in normal everyday contexts.

Social interaction cues

As we might predict from the arguments earlier in this chapter, normal social interaction can take place only because individuals have certain expectations about it (beliefs about how other people will act; assumptions about what may or may not be done in certain circumstances; inferences about what someone else is like). These hypotheses are, for all practical purposes, dependent on the many types of information the individual receives during interaction with others and on the ways he reacts to it. The parties to an interaction present each other with certain clear-cut physical cues (e.g. height, hair colour, shape) and other external cues (e.g. clothing, 'props' such as spectacles, umbrellas and brief cases). The centrality of such cues in social behaviour has been reviewed by Warr and Knapper (1968); and the complex of other factors relating to the interaction process is becoming increasingly apparent. One important variable, for example, is space usage (Hall, 1963; Sommer, 1965). Not only do people lay claim to possession of space in several direct and indirect ways — for example, by placing their name on the door of a room, or by hanging a coat over the back of a chair — they also indicate their control of the space by, for instance, placing their feet on a desk. They may indicate territorial rights even when they have left the space, e.g. by leaving open books on a library reading room table. Such examples represent the essentially *static* features of behaviour used to indicate control over space, and to convey (usually) the implication of higher status. Those controlling most space are those of highest rank — in ways often formally prescribed, as in the Civil Service and other institutions, where the size of room, desk and carpet is related to status most precisely. But there is also a *dynamic* element to space usage which in normal flowing sequences of social interaction is important in various ways.

For example (Argyle, 1975), people generally stand closer to people they like than to those they dislike; people stand or sit further away from others in highly formal encounters than they do in friendly or informal ones; people normally touch others (i.e. 'invade their closest space') only if they know one another well — and accidental touching of others has to be excused. During the flow of normal interactions, such distances and spatial relationships are carefully regulated (Argyle, 1969). Additionally, individuals interact with one another non-verbally by the way that they look at one another, smile, gesture and move round. The work of Argyle and his co-workers in general has shown that the significance of these activities in human social behaviour is paramount, particularly the manner by which one looks another person in the eye. Such 'eye contact' serves several purposes. Its basic function is simply that of gathering information: people look at their partner more often when they are alarmed, when something unexpected happens, or when they are suddenly stressed by the type of questions or tone of voice of the partner (Duck, 1974). But it may also convey information. At certain levels of intimacy and liking people look at one another more often; dominance or threat can be indicated by staring — and the threat conveyed in this way can often, as in the animal kingdom, be sufficient to induce flight and escape (Ellsworth, Carlsmith and Henson, 1972). The importance of eye contact in social interaction thus relates to the information it provides about one person's feelings for another both individually and reciprocally, and it permits individuals to establish expectancies about one another in these most basic respects. Even simple liking can be affected by the extremely subtle cue of variable pupil size: Hess (1965), for example, showed subjects two photographs of the same model: one showing the pupils dilated and one not. It was found that subjects preferred the photograph of the person with dilated pupils, for these themselves are a usual indicator that the other person likes what he is looking at.

Apparently insignificant though such cues may be individually, their potential effects are profound. A classic finding of the research on physical/external cues, for example, is that, on first impression, people who wear spectacles are judged to be more intelligent than people not wearing spectacles (Thornton, 1944). After periods of about five minutes spent in discussion the effects of this cue fade and are replaced by others (Argyle and McHenry, 1971); but in the 'maximum ambiguity' condition generally (previous section), the simple external cue of spectacles proves a sufficient basis for suppositions about a person's actual character and personality — and such cues are used, quite intentionally, by TV advertisers to lend credibility to their product. Thus headache powders are typically advertised by older men wearing spectacles and white coats, carrying a clipboard and writing with a fountain-pen — all of which cues are intended to make the actor using them appear more authoritative. The study of judgements regarding authoritativeness emerges as an important area of the present investigation (chapter 4), not simply because certain persuasive cues to authoritativeness may be deliberately abused, but because other cues are seen to influence the judgements of television viewers in this respect quite unwittingly.

For in normal social interaction non-verbal cueing has a further purpose: besides simply helping people to draw inferences it also helps them to sequence their behaviour. (Here we return to the important sequence factor of the previous section.) In normal conversation people take it in turn to speak in a manner that is far more complex than it appears on the surface. In order not to continually interrupt one another, conversants employ elaborate social 'rules' and codes which inform each of them when to speak and when to stay listening. Styles of eye contact, once again, have an important coded value in this respect. Most people are familiar with the fact that interactions begin when they 'catch someone's eye' — and barmen are equally familiar with the fact that people do not usually start interactions until eye contact is established. Moreover, once an interaction is begun, eye contact serves the important though less obvious regulating function (Argyle and Kendon, 1967) of signifying whether someone is at the end of his speech or still wishes to 'retain the floor'. (The phenomenon thus serves the phatic function discussed in chapter 2.) As the latter writers indicate, speakers tend to look away from a listener when they are developing a point, looking back only every so often in order to gather information on, for instance, how the point is being understood, whether they should elaborate it, or whether the listener is becoming bored. When the end of an utterance is reached, the speaker looks at his audience more steadily and thereby signals that the latter may start speaking himself. In fact, such information can also be conveyed by a range of cues, including smiling and nodding (which encourage the speaker to continue speaking), frowning (which may make him stop), and 'filled pauses' like 'um', 'er', 'you know', and 'I mean' (which indicate that the speaker, although temporarily halted in his tracks, has not finished saying what he wants to say and should not therefore be interrupted).

All of these codes need a certain amount of 'skilled' usage for normal interactions to run a proper course, and for the individual it is fundamentally important that the skills of phatic communication be effectively acquired. People who lack the skills necessary to maintain the acknowledged sequences of interpersonal behaviour are often thought to be, for example, shy, shifty or ashamed. (One popular TV comedian makes much of the fact that he expects others to 'look at me when I'm talking to you'.) At extreme ends of the continuum, people who show no phatic ability at all become impossible to deal with: when a person totally averts his gaze or, on the other hand, continually stares, people tend to withdraw from his company (Argyle, 1969). Moreover, it has been suggested that the inability to maintain proper forms of non-verbal contact may be a contributory factor in the development of certain types of schizophrenic withdrawal (E. Williams, 1974). Certainly — as hinted already — an intriguing feature of the non-verbal codes, known in analyses of language as 'paralinguistic' forms, is that they may quite dominate the verbal messages that they accompany:

> It seems to be the case that, whenever there is a contradiction between the overt form of the verbal part of an utterance and the associated prosodic or paralinguistic features, it is the latter which determine the semiotic or 'functional' classification of the utterance (as a question rather than a statement, as a tentative suggestion rather than a question, and so on). (Lyons, 1972, p.62)

Consequently, the effects of conflict between message theme and the functional cues of eye contact are indeed likely to be the same as the schizophrenic 'double-bind' effects of functional—thematic conflict indicated in chapter 2. And the significance of Lyons' observation in relation to the various functions of television becomes central at later stages of the book. Such is their power that the phatic features of interaction may frequently be used for the sole purpose of prolonging communication when there is nothing to say:

> Dorothy Parker caught eloquent examples: ' "Well!" the young man said. "Well!" she said. "Well, here we are," he said. "Here we are," she said. "Aren't we?" "I should say we were," he said. "Eeyop! Here we are." "Well!" she said. "Well!" he said, "well." ' (Jakobson, 1960, pp.355—6)

In this type of communication, Jakobson hints, man resembles the talking bird.

In normal social interaction, then, people are perpetually tuned in to a variety of cues that indicate how the interaction shall proceed, and on the basis of which they make some far-reaching assumptions about the nature and character of the person with whom they are interacting. Not only does this apply when they are dealing with someone personally; it also applies when they themselves are observers of an interaction between others. In this situation, additional cues regarding the relative position, posture and behaviour of the conversants come into play, enabling observers to deduce (1) the nature of the interaction, e.g. the relative status, liking and intimacy of the participants (Harré, in press); (2) the personality of each (Duck, in press); (3) the extent to which either person shows confidence or authority about his subject (Cook, in press); and (4) their own liking for the two participants (Duck, in press). In view of the critical importance of these phenomena, both in normal behaviour and the assessment of it, it is thus desirable that something like normality be retained in TV interactions (such as interviews) if the function for which they are intended is to be achieved. In television and film studios, however, things are actually quite different from normal and highly constrained. Studios are hot, urgent places where the individual becomes a cog in a remarkable machine. Indirect evidence suggests strongly that the influence of filming conditions on the behaviour viewed on television will be substantial — and the important point to establish is whether the viewer reacts to these distortions by forming equally distorted hypotheses about the people and situations he sees. Space usage, for example, both in studio and exterior conditions of filming, is predominantly determined by technical needs: thus, an interviewer and interviewee are often placed in unusual spatial relationships so that they can share a microphone or camera. Research on satisfaction with amounts of space allotted during interaction, however, shows that it is disruptive to force people to stand or sit closer than they would normally prefer. It is clear that individuals have 'body buffer zones' — areas of space around them that they do not like other people to 'invade' — and it is evident (Kane, 1973) that violent prisoners are often people who respond vigorously to 'body buffer zone invasions' *per se.* Similarly, Griffit and Veitch (1971) showed that cramped and hot conditions (TV studios fit this description) disrupt normal behaviour and increase anxiety, anger and the likelihood of hostility between those who interact within them. In TV conditions all of these factors may combine with an inexperienced interviewee's existing anxieties to cause him to behave in a somewhat distorted, unusual manner. The dynamic interaction in which he is involved takes place on the interviewer's terms — usually on his territory and featuring his 'props' (desk, chair, clipboard and other symbols of professional status). If the interview is conducted on the interviewee's territory — in his office or home — it speedily becomes the domain of the mediators by the introduction of cameras, arc lights, cables and the very fact that someone else (e.g. a director) tells him where to sit, which space to occupy and so forth. Whether or not the mediators are at pains to preserve normality in this respect, the extreme selectivity of the television image is likely to place its subject in precisely the type of void described earlier by Scheff's 'maximum ambiguity' situation, where the static cues to his character are either disguised or barred from the screen altogether. So, as the previous argument has shown, viewers in this situation are forced to form their judgements about the performer's personality, authority and reliability (as doctor, economist, professor, etc.) on the basis of more marginal clues.

The medium potentially has full control over all cues, for even in connection with his intended function in a programme, a speaker may be introduced to the audience in various explicit and implicit ways. As an explicit cue, his name may be presented on a caption with a sub-title giving his status; his record of service (as a politician, for example) may be described as he is introduced; or he may wear a uniform and a stethoscope around his neck. There are boundless possibilities for explicit audience cueing in this way. Far more insidious, however, is the possibility that implicit, unconscious cues may operate on the perception and interpretation of televised material as in any other human context. And in this respect we may consider a particular characteristic of television as advanced by its prime theorist. According to McLuhan (1967), television is a 'cool' medium, by which he means it is an involving, rather than a 'hot' or forceful medium (!). This rather strange theory is based on a premise that the low definition of the television picture requires its viewer to 'fill in' the gaps in the Gestaltist fashion mentioned earlier in the chapter: this act, McLuhan suggests, involves viewers in the image to the exclusion of its meaning. Both the Gestaltist hypothesis and its corollary are, of course, totally in tune with the present argument: the former emphasises the viewer's tendency to base his observations on meaningful patterns, while the latter indicates the possibility that message content and form may have separate effects. But McLuhan's linkage between them is both unfounded and distracting — as unfounded in general psychological knowledge as his theory of the 'global village' is in social psychological terms (Preface), and distracting because it forces us into the generalised position of regarding the properties of television as constant however its imagery is handled. There is no more basis for us to say that the form of a message and its meaning are (necessarily) separate than there is to suggest that the medium and the message are completely synonymous.

For slightly less subjective evidence regarding television's distorting properties, we must turn to more recent literature, and a piece of experimental work by McMenamin (1974). The ratings of a lecturer seen simultaneously 'live' and on closed-circuit television were shown tentatively by McMenamin to differ in terms of two personality factors: 'poised' and 'empathic'. The former emerges as a feature of the lecturer perceived by the audience in the face to face situation, and the latter as a feature of his televised performance. The main significance here is the simple indication that the two simultaneous conditions (TV and non-TV) elicit different perceptions of the same man. McMenamin's further interpretations of his data, however, are more questionable. Why, for example, do not the two factors — each a positive attribute in a lecturer — both manifest themselves in the same condition? McMenamin suggests that the subjects were unable to perceive poise on television, being 'in no position to challenge it', though one might still expect the two factors, if not supportive of one another, to have cancelled each other out. Why, also, should such sub-factors as being 'professional', 'dedicated', and 'educated' be interpreted as representative of an 'empathic' factor specifically? Evidently, this particular interpretation stems directly from McLuhan's 'hot and cool' theory, and inferentially it is as subjective as the McLuhan notion itself. As a basis for theory — or even the support of it — the investigation is clearly rather insubstantial; but it does serve as a tantalising indicator of possibilities.

For what could be the particular cues on which television's undoubted distorting capacity is based? Can they actually be identified at all? On the

66

hypothetical basis that television simply disturbs the social behaviour it presents (as we have seen, there is sufficient evidence for this to be the case), we may suppose television's distortions to arise at the face-value level of its subject matter in part at least. Additionally, from the evidence concerning the importance of sequential factors in perception and interpretation at all levels, we may suggest that television is disruptive whenever and in whatever form it presents sequential patterns of information (as via editing procedures) that are inconsistent with those the viewer perceives normally. On this basis he may form quite reliable conclusions about information to which his normal judgemental processes have led him, but which in normal contexts would be wholly incorrect. Rather than deliberately falsifying information, our case goes, television may unintentionally stress or conceal the very cues that viewers need for the assessments of a speaker's credibility in a particular function and context: and the distortion of the viewing experience in this respect stems from the medium's failure to reflect adequately the patterns found in 'real life'. Hitherto, it has been assumed that the interaction rules of normal social situations apply equally in the artificial context of mediated behaviour; and virtually no attention has been given by researchers to the possibility that the codes are different.

A counter-argument, however, is to suggest that the formal stylistics of television have by now become capable of interpretation by the viewer to the point where he may recognise the abnormal cues produced as artefacts of the medium and not to be used in the inferential process. This is undeniably true in certain ways. For example, a slow zoom-in on a particular player or setting is readily understood as emphasis of them, in both interpretation and intention alike, and conventional cutting styles (chapter 2) are intended to reflect, and are similarly interpreted as reflecting, the to and fro of normal conversation. In basic production manuals (Neads, 1976) the trainee producer is instructed to follow the mainstream of the action wherever possible, giving the alternate views of speakers one would normally expect. But of course rules are made for breaking, as indicated in the earlier 'stylistics and structure' discussion; and when a producer deliberately strives for certain unpredictable effects, many of the cues he provides will be open to misinterpretation. At this stage or any other it is thus impossible to resolve the question of the medium's distorting powers simply by a discussion of the total range of effects (intended or otherwise) that a producer may create: it is necessary to consider these effects in terms of the viewers' normal responses to the cues and signals they believe to have significance.

Levels of viewing involvement

In connection with educational broadcasting, Pendred (1976) has posed the question 'Is anybody there?'. In the use of television in education a common complaint is that equipment is purchased at great expense but then nobody watches it. Even when individuals actually do watch television, their viewing experiences may differ substantially, and an analysis of the individual viewing experience is thus only complete when the many levels at which the medium's effects may be exerted can be identified. As we have seen in the present chapter, the influence of many psychological cues to perception and interpretation may be quite unconscious; and when the effects of television are based at this level their identification certainly becomes problematic. But, as we have argued, the basis for all effects, conscious or otherwise, is the individual's ability to perceive a structure in the cues on which he can base hypotheses. If we can identify the types of structure that the television viewer perceives, therefore, the search for possible effects may be guided. If it is clear that the narrative of a television production has a structure that the viewer can clearly define as it develops, then an active level of involvement in the production may be predicted, and a number of positive effects indicated. If it is unlikely that the viewer can perceive a significant narrative structure in the material, then we must assume that his viewing experience is characterised by a less active involvement in the material, and that the TV images alone are commanding his attention.

But the actual imagery of television may in itself command the viewer's attention at different levels. When the producer's obvious aim is to provide a perceptual experience alone, the question we must ask is whether the viewing experience of an individual is actively based on the image cues or is quite passive. Accordingly, we may identify three possible levels of involvement in TV material: (1) the highest level, at which active involvement in the implications of the narrative occurs; (2) an intermediate level, at which active involvement in the implications of the visual/aural imagery alone occurs; and (3) the lowest level, at which there is a totally passive involvement in the imagery's simple novelty value. If the TV viewing experience is characterised by an active involvement in the narrative specifically, it is obviously dependent on the viewers' ability to actively interpret the aural and visual images he perceives. An appreciation of the imagery for aesthetic reasons, however, may be a totally sufficient basis for the viewing experience in itself — as may also be a totally passive perception of the imagery, in view of the immense satisfaction to be gained from basic perceptual arousal (chapter 2) — and, having clarified the relationship between TV subject matter and imagery to this extent, we may begin to consider the types of structure a viewer may perceive within each.

In the earlier discussion during this chapter of the effects of context on and within programme content, a primary structural factor influencing perception was that of sequence. If the sequence of TV messages is meaningful, the necessary structure for an individual's hypotheses is provided and the viewing experience is potentially active. If the sequence as presented to him is not logical, however, the viewer may nonetheless attempt to impose upon the material a logical (non-sequential) structure of his own. The analysis of structure in the viewing experience is thus an examination of both sequential and non-sequential types of logic; and the intended and interpreted structures of a message may differ in these terms. Greimas (1966) objects to the assumption by traditional content analysts that the internal sequence of messages in a narrative structure is perceived and interpreted in the same logical fashion that characterised it on transmission; and he indicates that the logical order of priority the receiver may place on a set of messages may bear little resemblance to the linear sequence in which they were originally expressed. According to Greimas, the analysis of message forms must therefore seek a logical structure within the message that is independent of its chronology; (unfortunately the method he proposes for this purpose assumes the existence of an absolute, universal textual form lying outside the message, against which specific texts may be tested — and this is a notion which, as we have argued in chapter 2, is not susceptible to proof). In a discussion of the viewing experience generally, however, the argument against assumptions of linearity in the message analysis is particularly important. For there is certainly much on television that seems either unconcerned with the clear exposition of its subject matter or bent on making the viewer's construction of it difficult. When we inspect the linear sequence of elements in an evening, for example — a global 'viewing experience' for a substantial proportion of the population (see below) — or even within many single programmes, we may easily realise that the viewer cannot possibly interpret the complex sequence which is presented in an integrated logical fashion. He may be selective within that context, perceiving meaningful effects on an occasional basis, but many elements that he perceives will fit into no logical structure at all. When the elements that television presents are well integrated, as in a tightly knit play (and as the full evening's viewing, being eclectic, is not), the viewing experience may plausibly be characterised by an active level of involvement throughout. Otherwise an active level of involvement may be possible on a selective basis; and by extension we see that the passive viewing experience is by definition that which is quite unselective. For a television viewer the effort to find meaning thus consists in making systematic connections between the message elements he has sampled according to his ongoing interpretation of the whole.

The frequent aim of making the logical structure of television content difficult for the viewer to construct may be seen in the analysis of TV dramatic sequences. Via the continual slicing and parallel structuring of the action and various film locations, most thriller narratives gain their attraction by preventing the viewer from understanding the logic of their sequence until the final denouement. While the reader of a book may clarify his interpretation of its contents by turning back and forth as he pleases at the pace he most prefers, television content grants no such favours and the viewer must cope with its complexity as best he can. The classic *Perry Mason* cases progressed remorselessly towards a situation in which the famous attorney discovered the real culprit via a well laid out logical scheme known to him alone. For the viewers' benefit the television episodes thus ended with the inevitable enquiry by Della Street: 'But what I want to know, Perry, is how you knew that . . .?'. More recently the thriller model on television has been modified considerably. In *Columbo* the real culprit is known to the viewer all the time: the question is whether this is equally clear to the detective and the precise way in which blame will eventually be proved: we trust there is a hidden scheme to things and in the end we are proved right. The tension of television drama derives specifically in this way — from the understanding that the dramatist is one step ahead of us — and the 'non-transparency' of its structure is the drama's essence.

The supreme example of a dramatic structure whose logic is kept a dark (opaque) secret, at the end often remaining so, is *Mission Impossible.* In this most ingenious of series, the undercover agents work towards the accomplishment of their mission using a baffling sequence of subterfuge that the viewers may only unravel if they are willing to do so in retrospect during their own time. It is extremely doubtful whether even the actors understand what they are doing, for to penetrate the programme's logic one must start at the denouement, reverse the linear sequence which has led up to it, and assess the elements of the narrative in their new-found context. But since the significance of the elements was not necessarily apparent when they were originally presented, it is unlikely that many of them will be recalled; and the fascination of such a programme stems precisely from the viewer's sense of a secret that is too great for sharing. *Mission Impossible* is therefore a prime example of television designed to promote an involvement in imagery and spectacle rather than an active intellectual attention to the narrative. The assumptions of previous research (that media content comes over to the viewer in pristine fashion, and is logically interpreted even in the short term) is clearly quite incapable of general application. We are forced to conclude that much of the viewing experience — when it spans long periods in particular — is indeed a quite docile acquiescence in the undoubted attractions of television's imagery alone.

The quite mesmeric ability of television to capture our attention from one programme to the next, even against our wishes, is central to our argument regarding the power of the TV image in general. When television material no longer concerns us, we do not necessarily leave the room, look away because we are not interested, or switch off: for the viewing experience is evidently sufficiently impelling to keep us intrigued in the absence of better things to do. It is possible to sit down with the intention of watching a specific programme only, and to find oneself four hours later viewing the end of the evening's transmission: one has been caught in a 'flow' of programmes and programme imagery which one had no previous intention of viewing and, having done so, does not recall. (Indeed the assumption that this is so underlies much programme planning, cf. chapter 2.) The 'flow' condition itself has been discussed by R. Williams (1974):

> ... for the fact is that many of us do sit there and much of the critical significance of television must be related to this fact. I know that whenever I tried [as a TV critic] to describe the experience of flow, on a particular evening or more generally, what I could say was unfinished and tentative, yet I learned from correspondence that I was engaging with an experience which many viewers were aware of and were trying to understand. There can be 'classical' kinds of response, at different levels, to some though not all of the discrete units. But we are only just beginning to recognise, let alone solve, the problems of description and response to the facts of flow. (pp.95–6)

An important step in the investigation of viewing behaviour in this respect has been made by Goodhardt, et al. (1975). In an analysis of viewing figures collected for the Independent Broadcasting Authority over the eight-year period from 1967 to 1975, they have examined in detail programming assumptions made regarding viewing intensity, flow, channel loyalty and repeat viewing. In the immediate context of our own enquiry, they indicate that the model of 'an evening's viewing' is, for 55 per cent of the population at least, an appropriate expression of one type of viewing experience. (At this, as at other levels, we argue that the experience may thus be characterised psychologically in terms of its perceived structure; according to both intention and interpretation, an evening's viewing is bound to be eclectic: it is evidently a compelling but unselective experience.) The remaining 45 per cent of the audience however, is more selective, typically using television for more specific reasons. For them the compulsion of a whole evening's viewing is easily outweighed by temptations to spend the evening, or part of it, otherwise. Whether the reasons for continuous viewing across an (eclectic) evening's output are preference or pure circumstance, it is unlikely that the prime reason is an interest in thematic content alone:

> ... people with a real specialist interest do not generally feel a need to follow it *on television*. Artists do not feel they need to watch art programmes: knitters, knitting programmes; or business men, business programmes ... Specialists already know all that. Even religious people do not religiously watch all their programmes, but go to Church instead. (Goodhardt et al., 1975, p.131)

Of course, being experts in marketing, rather than psychology, Goodhardt et al. do not go beyond their data to posit the bases and determinants of television's impact. They are not therefore concerned to say whether the strangely constant 55 per cent that recurs within their data is — as an estimate of the viewing population that watches television in a docile, passive fashion — particularly large; or whether the remaining 45 per cent of viewers who are more selective in their viewing preferences constitute a surprisingly small group. In terms of previous research assumptions, we would suggest that both the passivity and disloyalty of viewers to TV material are surprisingly high: they certainly confirm our suspicions regarding the inadequacy of the traditional content analytic approach; and (at 55 per cent) they emphasise the strength of the 'flow' condition specifically. (In programme scheduling terms, of course, the same statistic reflects the success of policies designed to increase flow — cf. chapter 2 — and, to the schedulers, 55 per cent may thus be disappointingly low.)

In the next chapter we test out the hypothesis that the origin of these phenomena, in part at least, may be the unwitting and unconscious effects of presentation factors alone. Of course, in order to demonstrate whether this is likely, we need to find a way in which the effects of the TV image may be determined quite independently of those relating to the subject matter it conveys. Accordingly, we report a series of experiments in which presentation strategy was varied, while all content variables not under examination were held carefully constant. The specific hypothesis under test may be phrased as follows: that when we are gripped by the television phenomenon at a less than active level of involvement, is it not the simple images alone — the movement, the shapes, the changes of shot and the juxtaposition of one image and the next — that we are often heeding, with no specific orientation to the information conveyed at all?

Summary

(1)   Perception of any stimulus is a complex constructive activity involving motivational and cognitive factors as well as those pertaining to the stimulus itself. The determinist approach to media overlooks the individual differences in perception, and their dynamic variability.

(2)   The interpretation of a stimulus is based on attitudes to, for example, its credibility and visual interest. These attitudes are in turn based on specific perceptual cues.

(3)   The simultaneous and sequential context in which a stimulus is perceived influences interpretation of its meaning. The effects of TV subject matter, therefore, can only be understood in relation to the manner in which it is presented.

(4)   The cues emitted and perceived in normal social interaction have a coded significance that aids the participants to deal with one another appropriately. Television situations frequently disturb the normal patterns of behaviour by presenting the viewer with abnormal cues and causing him to make distorted interpretations.

(5)   The effects of TV content are ultimately determined by the viewers' level of involvement in it. The phenomena of 'flow' reveal that a high proportion of TV viewing is passive and unselective, evidently motivated by an interest in the imagery of the medium alone.

References

Argyle, M. (1967), *The Psychology of Interpersonal Behaviour*, Harmondsworth, Penguin.

Argyle, M. (1969), *Social Interaction*, London, Methuen.

Argyle, M. (1975), *Bodily Communication*, London, University Paperbacks.

Argyle, M. and Kendon, A. (1967), 'The experimental analysis of social performance', in Berkowitz, L. (ed.), *Advances in Experimental Social Psychology,* vol. 3, New York, Academic Press.

Argyle, M. and McHenry, R. (1971), 'Do spectacles really affect judgements of intelligence?', *Brit. J. Soc. Clin. Psychol.,* vol. 10.

Bannister, D. and Mair, J. M. (1968), *The Evaluation of Personal Constructs,* London, Academic Press.

Bartlett, F. C. (1932), *Remembering,* Cambridge, Cambridge University Press.

Beams, H. L. (1954), 'Affectivity as a factor in the apparent size of pictured food objects', *J. Exp. Psychol.,* vol. 47.

Bexton, W. H., Heron, W. and Scott, T. H. (1954), 'Effects of decreased variation in the sensory environment', *Can. J. Psychol.,* vol. 8.

Brand, C. (1973), paper read to the Scottish Branch of the British Psychological Society.

Bruner, J. S. and Postman, L. (1947a), 'Tension and tension release as organising factors in perception', *J. Person.,* vol. 15.

Bruner, J. S. and Postman, L. (1947b), 'Emotional selectivity in perception and reaction', *J. Person.,* vol. 16.

Bruner, J. S. and Postman, L. (1948), 'Symbolic value as an organising factor in perception', *J. Soc. Psychol.,* vol. 27.

Cook, M. (in press), 'The social skill model and interpersonal attraction', in Duck, S. W. (ed.), *Theory and Practice in Interpersonal Attraction,* London, Academic Press.

DeCharms, R., Carpenter, V. and Kuperman, A. (1965), 'The "origin-pawn" variable in person perception', *Sociometry,* vol. 28.

Duck, S. W. (1973), *Personal Relationships and Personal Constructs: A Study of Friendship Formation,* London, Wiley.

Duck, S. W. (1974), 'Frequency of eye contact as a function of stress and strength of relationship', *IRCS Research on Psychology,* 2.

Duck, S. W. (in press), 'Tell me where is fancy bred: some thoughts on the study of interpersonal attraction', in Duck, S. W. (ed.), *Theory and Practice in Interpersonal Attraction,* London, Academic Press.

Duck, S. W. and Baggaley, J. P. (1975a), 'Audience reaction and its effect on perceived expertise', *Communication Research,* vol. 2, no. 1.

Ellsworth, P. C., Carlsmith, J. M. and Henson, A. (1972) 'The stare as a stimulus to flight in human subjects: a series of field experiments', *J. Pers. Soc. Psychol.,* vol. 21.

Eysenck, H. J. and Eysenck, S. B. G. (1964), *Manual: Eysenck Personality Inventory,* London, University of London Press.

Farina, A., Allen, J. G. and Saul, B. B. B. (1968), 'The role of the stigmatised person in affecting social relationships', *J. Person.*, vol. 36.

Festinger, L. (1954), 'The theory of social comparison processes', *Human Relations*, vol. 7.

Goodhardt, G. J., Ehrenberg, A. S. C. and Collins, M. A. (1975), *The Television Audience: Patterns of Viewing*, Farnborough, Saxon House.

Gough, H. (1958), *Manual: California Psychological Inventory*, Palo Alto, CPP.

Gregory, R. L. (1966), *Eye and Brain*, London, WUL.

Greimas, A. J. (1966), *La Semantique Structurale*, Paris, Larousse.

Griffit, W. and Veitch, R. (1971), 'Hot and crowded: influences of population density and temperature on interpersonal behaviour', *J. Pers. Soc. Psychol.*, vol. 17.

Hall, E. T. (1963), 'A system for the notation of proxemic behaviour', *Amer. Anthropol.*, vol. 65.

Harré, R. (in press), 'Friendship as an accomplishment: the ethogenic approach to interpersonal attraction', in Duck, S. W. (ed.), *Theory and Practice in Interpersonal Attraction*, London, Academic Press.

Harris, P. L. (1975), 'The development of search and object permanence', *Psych. Bull.*, vol. 82.

Heron, W., Doane, B. K. and Scott, T. H. (1956), 'Visual disturbances after prolonged perceptual isolation', *Can. J. Psych.*, vol. 10.

Hess, E. H. (1965), 'Attitude and pupil size', *Scientific American*, no. 212.

Hovland, C. I., Lumsdaine, A. and Sheffield, F. D. (1949), *Experiments on Mass Communication*, Princeton, New Jersey, Princeton University Press.

Hovland, C. I. and Mandell, W. (1952), 'An experimental comparison of conclusion-drawing by the communicator and by the audience', *J. Abn. Soc. Psychol.*, vol. 47.

Hovland, C. I. and Weiss, W. (1952), 'The influence of source credibility on communication effectiveness', *Public Opinion Quarterly*, 15.

Jakobson, R. (1960), 'Linguistics and poetics', in Sebeok, T. A. (ed.), *Style in Language*, Cambridge, Mass., MIT Press.

Kane, J. (1973), 'Body Buffer Zones in Violent Prisoners', unpublished MA project, Glasgow University.

Kelley, H. H. (1950), 'The warm—cold variable in first impressions of persons', *J. Person.*, vol. 18.

Kelley, H. H. and Woodruff, C. L. (1956), 'Members' reactions to apparent group approval of a counter-norm communication', *J. Abn. Soc. Psychol.*, vol. 52.

Kelly, G. A. (1955), *The Psychology of Personal Constructs*, New York,

Norton.

Kelman, H. C. and Hovland, C. I. (1953), ' "Reinstatement" of the communicator in delayed measurement of opinion change', *J. Abn. Soc. Psychol.*, vol. 48.

Koffka, K. (1935), *Principles of Gestalt Psychology*, New York, Harcourt Brace Jovanovich.

Landy, D. (1972), 'The effects of an overheard audience's reaction and attractiveness on opinion change', *J. Exp. Soc. Psychol.*, vol. 8.

Levy, L. H. (1960), 'Context effects in social perception', *J. Abn. Soc. Psychol.*, vol. 61.

Lyons, J. (1972), 'Human language', in Hinde, R. A. (ed.), *Non-Verbal Communication*, Cambridge, Cambridge University Press.

McLuhan, M. (1967), *The Medium is the Message*, New York, McGraw-Hill.

McMenamin, M. J. (1974), 'Effect of instructional television on personality perception', *AV Communication Review*, vol. 22, no. 1.

Mascaro, G. F. and Graves, W. (1973), 'Contrast effects of background factors on the similarity–attraction relationship', *J. Pers. Soc. Psychol.*, vol. 25.

Mitchell, H. E. and Byrne, D. (1973), 'The defendant's dilemma: effects of juniors' attitudes and authoritarianism on judicial decisions', *J. Pers. Soc. Psychol.*, vol. 25.

Neads, C. (1976), 'TV production – a student guide', *Journal of Educational Television*, vol. 2, no. 1.

Newman, H. F., Freeman, F. N. and Holzinger, K. J. (1937), *Twins: A Study of Heredity and Environment*, Chicago, University of Chicago Press.

Orne, M. and Scheibe, K. E. (1964), 'The contribution of non-deprivation factors in the production of sensory deprivation effects: the psychology of the "panic button" ', *J. Abn. Soc. Psychol.*, vol. 68.

Pendred, P. (1976), 'Excuse me – is anybody there?', paper read to the International Conference on Evaluation and Research in Educational Broadcasting, Open University.

Postman, L. and Egan, J. P. (1949), *Experimental Psychology*, New York, Harper.

Robbins, G. E. (1975), 'Dogmatism and information gathering in personality impression formation', *J. Research in Personality*, vol. 9.

Scheff, T. J. (1973), 'Intersubjectivity and emotion', *Amer. Behav. Scientist*, vol. 16.

Sommer, R. (1965), 'Further studies of small group ecology', *Sociometry*, vol. 28.

Thornton, G. R. (1944), 'The effect of wearing glasses on judgements of personality traits of people seen briefly', *J. App. Psychol.*, vol. 28.

Warr, P. and Knapper, C. (1968), *The Perception of People and Events*, London, Wiley.

Williams, E. (1974), 'An analysis of gaze in schizophrenics', *Brit. J. Soc. Clin. Psychol.*, vol. 13.

Williams, R. (1974), *Television: Technology and Cultural Form*, London, Fontana.

4 The reflected image

In the title to this chapter we have consciously used the word 'image' in two senses: firstly with respect to the physical images television conveys, and secondly with respect to the conceptual 'image' an individual or social group acquires in the minds of others (chapter 1). Our case henceforward is that, even when more reliable sources of information about him are available (e.g. his words and opinions), a TV performer's public image may be based solely on the visual images that mediate him. To this extent it is correct that use of the term should be ambiguous.

For in the previous chapter we examined the overwhelming evidence in the socio-psychological literature that the individual, when receiving information, makes critical use of its non-verbal elements in deciding how to interpret its actual verbal significance. When the verbal and non-verbal content of TV material come into conflict with each other, it may certainly be predicted – in keeping with the linguistic and psychological literature we have discussed (e.g. Lyons, 1972; Argyle, 1975) – that the lasting effects on the viewer are likely to be those of the non-verbal elements exclusively, the imagery of television that stems from the presentation techniques producers use. In fact, recent evidence that viewers' attention to the verbal significance of TV material is far less than has previously been assumed (R. Williams, 1974; Goodhardt et al., 1975) leads us to suppose that the mediating techniques of television may be the root of even more insistent effects. In the present chapter we explore this possibility.

We describe a series of experiments in which simple factual material was reported or discussed on videotape. A number of TV production techniques commonly used in such situations were examined separately and in combination. The verbal content and image content of the material were always supportive – relevant to one another – for we were concerned to establish whether presentation variables affect viewers' reactions to the subject matter of TV material even when there is no apparent conflict between them. Where can such effects be predicted to settle, and what aspects of viewing response are they likely to attack? Previous research has shown the basic tendency on the part of those who receive a message to seek bases – even of the most tenuous kind – on which to assess the credibility of its source. Consequently, by personifying the message source in each of our experiments here via a studio performer, we have tested the hypothesis that the techniques used in presenting him or her contribute to the viewers' perception of those characteristics related to his credibility in particular. Our main purpose was therefore not simply to confirm that TV presentation techniques exert the effect on the viewer for which they are intended — increasing the visual impact of material, its novelty and variety, etc. — but to establish whether they have psychological effects that a producer would be unlikely to predict. A subsidiary aim was thus to compare the effects predicted according to the 'visual interest' criterion (chapter 2) with any other effects that might be evinced.

Physical image and conceptual image: some initial hypotheses

It is clear both from common sense and from much of the research discussed earlier (chapter 3) that if a source of information is rendered either more or less credible in itself, then so is the information stemming from it. It is surprising therefore that there has been hardly any research into this important point in the context of TV presentation. Given the range of effects outlined in the previous chapter, it is clear that there may be a whole series of ways in which the image of a TV performer can be formulated on the most superficial of bases, and his credibility in a particular function enhanced or diminished both intentionally and unintentionally. If this proves so, it clearly follows that the impact upon the viewing public of the performer's contribution is affected correspondingly. Evidence of this effect would certainly be most important in the context of news reporting and specialist correspondence where the viewer, having no expert knowledge in the area, is placed in the condition of 'maximum ambiguity' described by Scheff (1973), and becomes reliant on more marginal indices of performer credibility, as discussed earlier.

Paradoxically, the most difficult performances to give on television are, for many people, not the unscripted but the scripted ones, solo (reportive) presentations rather than group discussive ones. Even when the performer's verbal material is carefully memorised or presented to him via a prompting device, he may find particular problems in trying to behave before the camera in a manner that appears natural: these may be exacerbated by the very fact that the verbal delivery is not spontaneous. And since the non-verbal codes of the TV performance situation are characteristically so artificial in themselves (chapter 3), it is clear that actual distortions in the performance may be a prime source of viewing disturbance. Consequently, the credibility of a TV performer hangs greatly on his ability to project a deliberate self-image, behaving in an appropriate manner notwithstanding the constraints of the situation just as an actor does on stage. From this it is apparent that expertise on television is of two types. For an individual to be expert in the academic, technical or practical aspects of his subject matter is actually less critical when he appears on television than it is for him to be skilled in the art of self-projection. Secondly, it follows that anyone skilled in the latter art may give the impression that he is expert in the former sense also, and may actually acquit the role of 'subject specialist' better than the genuine article. In the unbiased, maximally efficient transmission of news and information on television, of course, it is extremely important (1) for the expert who is not an actor to be presented to the viewer in a manner that reflects his actual merits; and (2) that the actor who is not an expert should always be recognised as such. These questions, it will be noted, relate to presentation technique pure and simple: the immaculate verbal logic of a performance may be to no avail if its credibility is not also reflected in the performance itself. And in the assessment of television's impact henceforward it is thus exceedingly important that the dynamic effects of its presentation stylistics should receive immediate attention.

From the previous chapter it is also clear that the impact of a TV performance does not derive simply from the properties of the behaviour depicted, but in part from the ways in which the medium itself emphasises the natural sequences of social behaviour, and gives the viewer cues which permit him to respond to the behaviour as he would in normal social interactions. Clearly there is no need to prove that viewers do indeed respond to the cues they observe on television with the subtlety that characterises human responses in general: or that they do not form expectancies about what they see on TV just as they do in all other real life situations. The guiding hypothesis in the discussion that follows is thus that expectancies concerning a TV performance and the subsequent interpretation of it are derived by viewers from TV content at a number of levels. It is predicted that the sensitivity of the human observer to the marginal detail around him is so subtle that distortions produced when information is mediated in the rich visual terms of television may well be quite unintentional, and their origins undisclosed to viewer and producer alike.

What predictions can we therefore make regarding the source of these distortions? In the knowledge that cues to perceived credibility are those which are socially bizarre in even the minutest of ways, we may point, for instance, to the possible effects of those undoubted little jerky movements of the head made by newsreaders and others who are required to stare directly into the camera whilst they are talking. In part this behaviour may be due to the fact that it can usefully disguise the eye movements necessary to read the teleprompter machine, but it may also be due to the disruptive effects of speaking to a 'face' (i.e. to a camera) that does not give the important feedback that is customary in normal interaction. The difficulty with which inexperienced performers speak directly to a camera and 'hold a conversation with it' has been explained in these terms by Baggaley and Duck (1975b); and it is evident that a good deal of performing skill is necessary if audience reactions to a direct to camera performance are not to be jeopardised. We may thus argue (cf. Baggaley and Duck, 1975d) that the full face shot of a performer may actually lead to less favourable assessments of his credibility than a profile shot. On the other hand, Raban (1975) suggests that the very 'directness' of the straight address at camera has connotations of its own. As the most basic of television shots, he argues, the full face 'talking head' shot is of itself 'factual and authoritative', whereas a speaker 'framed in half-profile, talking away from the camera to a reporter' is likely to appear less so. 'The angle from which the picture is shot', Raban maintains, 'is enough to remind us that his words are partial'.

Naturally the tremendous wealth of factors underlying assessments of a speaker's image prevents us from ever predicting either effect with complete certainty. Clearly, speed of delivery, posture, gesture and sundry other variables, verbal and non-verbal, may all have interacting effects on such assessments, and deserve research attention in their own right. In the present experiments, however, these are not the central concern, and thus require rigorous control. (They are of course relatively easy effects to predict, while the effects of visual mediation alone are less obvious and therefore of greater immediate interest.) In the general fund of mediating techniques that we have already examined, there are several other variables we may predict to exert similar observable effects. The device whereby speakers are customarily portrayed against a 'relevant' back-ground, for instance: this may be predicted to exert far more subtle effects on the performance than on its visual interest alone. Work by Canter, West and Wools (1974) suggests that the type of room in which a person is viewed can in itself act as a context supplying the observer with actual cues to his status and ability (the importance of static cues to credibility in this way has been discussed at length in the previous chapter. The background of bookshelves against which an academic or politician may be presented on TV may consequently exude implications far more extensive than even the producer imagines. (The main implication of a bookshelf setting is that the performer actually reads some of the contents: he is clearly a thinking, rational man, whose message is going to be worth listening to.) The connotations are similar in the presentation of any visual cues – e.g. hand-held notes – or context which is relevant to the performer's function. If he is a physicist he is well-advised to stand in front of laboratory equipment; if he is a BBC science correspondent reporting from London about conditions on the back of the moon he is equally well-advised to present his report against a studio moonscape. The TV producer can rest assured that whatever implication he actually has in mind in using such techniques will be suitably elaborated by the viewer.

A further set of predictions regarding the effects of presentation on the performer's image may be generated in relation to the editing techniques commonly used in interview filming. When the question and answer sequence presented to the viewer is created according to film editing criteria rather than as an accurate reflection of the natural interaction that took place, the interpretation of the exchange may be distorted quite radically (Duck and Baggaley, 1975b). In their response to the sequential factors of human interaction, viewers are, as we have seen, extremely suggestible, and if, from one point in a conversation to the next, the behaviour of either participant does not match what the viewer expects, his perceptions of both will be affected. For example, a lack of appropriate interviewer shots may cause the film editor to 'cut away' to a shot of him smiling at a point where such a response seems entirely inappropriate; or one performer may seem to look in the opposite direction to that in which the other is pointing. Either way, the illusion of the interaction between them breaks down, and it can be predicted that the disruption caused by manipulation of the interviewer's role in a filmed interview alone may not only influence his own image, but also that of the interviewee and the credibility of the whole production. In view of the additional fact that the interviewer's role in the discussion may in itself be distorted by the demands upon him to repeat his questions into thin air, and to simulate reactions of approval or interest *in vacuo*, it is clear that the range of cues liable to affect viewing reaction to the message is immense (see the effects of facial expression and eye contact discussed by Argyle, 1969; E. Williams, 1974; and Duck and Baggaley, 1975b. (It has indeed been reported to the authors by a well-known TV interviewer that if the respondent departs at the point when 'cutaway' shots are required, she habitually asks a film crewman to stand in for him, so that she can re-enact her role in the discussion more comfortably.) And it is clear that when the edited cutaway shots indicate reactions of actual approval to what is being said, their impact is likely to be enhanced even more (cf. the work of Kelley and Woodruff (1956) reported in chapter 3).

The effects of such factors in TV performance may thus be of quite profound significance — and the need for close investigation is now indicated. Having laid the foundations of an empirical study by indicating the diversity of hypotheses that may be tested, we report the six experiments designed for this purpose. It is important to emphasise that each of the experiments was aimed primarily at establishing that a particular range of effects in TV presentation can and does take place; and the emphasis we lay upon the effects of presentation on the image of TV reporters and lecturers specifically is actually only one of several that we might have adopted in this respect. The experiments do not, therefore, claim to be exhaustive, nor do we suppose our results to indicate the relative efficiency of particular production techniques in general terms. The effects we report *are unique to the particular contexts from which they are derived* and the use of these techniques in other production contexts henceforward may yield entirely different results. The very dynamism of television's impact prevents the kind of data we report from being totally predictive *per se* — though we do claim that, as evidence for the hitherto neglected effects of presentation pure and simple, they are conclusive.

Six experiments: design and materials

Selection of variables

From the vast range of TV production procedures in use, a representative sample was selected for study. From the previous discussion it is clear that the types of procedure likely to exert particular effects on the viewer are those which, wittingly or not, provide *contextual cues* to judgements of the performer. The particular selection of presentation variables that we predicted would be capable of exerting such effects was as follows:

(1)   Variation of camera angle to show marginal detail (e.g. the performer's use of notes);
(2)   Addition of a visual background to a performer;
(3)   Variation of 'talking head' angles (front view vs profile);
(4)   Reactions of a television audience; and
(5)   Reactions of an interviewer.

Five experiments were designed to test the effects of these variables on perceptions of the performer specifically, though the implicit reactions to his verbal material were also considered. In a sixth experiment, a multivariate comparison of the five previous variables in combination was made, since only in interaction are TV techniques to be observed normally.

Preparation of videotapes

In order to investigate the effects of each presentation variable empirically, it was necessary to prepare videotape material in which the variable in question was manipulated; contrasting versions of the material were then presented each to a different audience of experimental subjects. In the first five experiments, dealing with one variable at a time, only two different versions of a presentation were required; in the final multivariate experiment, however, six versions were needed, each for presentation to a different audience in the usual manner. In order that any experimental effects observed could clearly be attributed to the manipulated variable alone, it was necessary for the actual performances (and thus subject matter) presented to the different audiences to be identical, with the contrasting versions recorded either using several cameras simultaneously, or created by an editing technique. The latter method requires that special care be taken to ensure that precisely the same lengths of 'insert' are edited into the standard material at precisely the same points in each version; only thus may one guarantee that no extraneous variables are introduced.

Whilst rigorously purist, such an approach is vital to an assessment of precise TV effects in this and any other connection, for the stimulus array presented on a TV screen is so complex that, as we have seen, any number of behavioural and contextual factors may modify viewers' assessments of it unless proper controls are exercised. One of the faults of much work on the effects of media content generally has been that different investigators have used different empirical criteria – witness the studies of TV violence (cf. Howitt and Cumberbatch, 1975). Thus in the latter context, some count only apparent murder and mayhem: some include *Tom and Jerry*; others count TV news reports, etc. Moreover, numerous different criteria for 'influence upon audiences' have been applied; some investigators use sociological data about increases in crime rates, while others use immediate post-experimental criteria. It is hardly surprising that the results of such studies are equivocal, ambiguous and unconvincing: a lesson certainly to be heeded by those wishing to examine the particular effects of media in isolation, as here.

A researcher wishing to measure subjects' reactions to any stimulus is faced with several choices: he can ask subjects to describe their experiences freely; he can provide the subjects with some questionnaire material; he can attempt to measure their change in attitudes; or he can give various behavioural tests which indicate subjects' future action tendencies (Aronson and Carlsmith, 1968). Each of these methods has advantages and disadvantages, but the one broad type of measure that suits our present methodology is one whereby subjects' descriptions of what they see is measured by means of adjectival scales. The scales most widely used for this purpose are based on the semantic differential technique developed by Osgood, Suci and Tannenbaum (1967). In full versions of this test the subject indicates his attitude to a person or object by rating it on a series of bipolar scales ranging between the extremes of one and seven, in which the 'undecided' or mid-point is represented by the score of four; either extreme may express the positive or negative pole of a particular scale as desired. Such scales may then be analysed in several ways. A common procedure is to divide the whole test into three main components, comprising scales measuring the evaluation of attitude objects (e.g. good–bad), its activity (e.g. active–passive) and potency (e.g. strong–weak); one may then assess the relative extents to which each component contributes to the subjects' assessments as a whole. A further method, often combined with the above, is to derive a visual representation of the subjects' ratings on each scale – a type of semantic graph. In the present research, comparisons were made in precisely this manner, on each individual scale of a semantic differential test between the ratings given by one experimental audience and those given by the other(s): the mean scores for each audience were then compared statistically. This procedure (more fully described in the appropriate sections below) permits a comparative estimate as to whether each group's responses on that particular scale have been significantly modified by the experimental manipulation in question.

While the semantic differential is not the only technique that could have been adopted in this connection, its proven utility in several spheres of social psychology (and particularly that area concerned, as here, with perception of other people – Warr and Knapper, 1968) is ample justification for its selection. It is easily administered and easily analysed and permits the selective testing of hypotheses in several ways. Firstly, the ability to assess the relative contribution of evaluation, activity or potency factors allows the researcher to identify the particular area of a subject's thinking that is most affected. Secondly, the inclusion of presumably 'irrelevant' scales in each category can permit him to establish whether the experimental variables affect a subject's assessments indiscriminately or more specifically. The adoption of this technique by other workers in this area in future can only improve the comparability of results found by different researchers and will thus contribute to the development of a paradigmatic approach to the problems we are tackling.

Individual effects of image variation

Experiment 1: use of notes The first experiment was designed to establish whether even visual cues apparently quite irrelevant to a performance may unwittingly affect judgements of it. A commonly used 'prop' of the TV performer is the set of notes which guides him through the programme. In some circumstances these may indeed be essential to his performance, while in others (e.g. the news, where the content is actually read from a cueing device at the camera lens) they are provided more for stand-by purposes. In recent years, viewers of television news have certainly become accustomed to seeing the readers referring to their script only occasionally; only at the end of the transmission are the sheets openly brandished, as the performer tidies them up 'for something to do'. In general terms the truly authoritative person, however, is clearly someone who uses no notes at all, and we may predict that in an informative context even such a marginal detail as the use of notes may serve circumstantially to cue perceptions of a person's actual ability.

In order to test this hypothesis, a three-minute lecture-type item was televised on the subject of Edgar Allan Poe. Two recordings of the lecture were made simultaneously using two cameras placed side by side with approximately thirty centimetres separating the lenses. The recordings were identical except for a slight variation in camera angle. The lecturer sat at ease in a plain studio setting and delivered his material *extempore*. By addressing the mid-point between the lenses he appeared to speak to both directly. He was also instructed to vary this technique and to look away from the cameras at occasional intervals. In so doing he effectively treated the cameras as another person to whom continuous eye contact is never given unwaveringly even during direct conversation (Argyle and Kendon, 1967, and chapter 3).

While one camera framed the speaker centrally the other framed him more to the left of the picture, bringing into vision the sheet of notes on his knee. The focal length of the two cameras was the same and the shot

Table 4.1

Experiment 1: Mean ratings of a lecturer seen (+) with notes and (o) without notes

	1	2	3	4	5	6	7		t	$p<$
Cautious		o	- - -	+				Rash	1·598	
Fair			o	- - -	+			Unfair	2·647	0·01
Unpleasant				o	- - +			Pleasant	0·663	
Expert			o	- - - +				Inexpert	1·073	
Undependable				+ o				Dependable	0·491	
Precise			o	- - -	+			Imprecise	0·910	
Evasive			+ - o					Direct	0·620	
Cold		+ - o						Warm	0·773	
Sincere			o	- - - +				Insincere	1·056	
Shallow				+ o				Profound	0·000	
Rational			o +					Intuitive	0·542	
Weak		+ - o						Forceful	0·772	
Kind			+ - o					Cruel	1·069	
Confusing	+ - - - - - - o							Straightforward	2·580	0·01

N.B. At $df = 20$, $t_{0.05} = 1·725$

remained fixed throughout the three minutes. The two recordings were each shown to separate student audiences (numbering eleven persons, none of whom knew the performer) and their assessments of him were obtained by the semantic differential technique described in the previous section. The adjectival scales used and the viewers' ratings of the performer on them are given in Table 4.1.

Viewers of the tape indicating the speaker's access to notes found him significantly less fair and more confusing than the viewers who did not see the notes. Since both audiences saw and heard precisely the same performance, the difference in their assessments of his ability as a lecturer can only derive from this most superficial of cues about him. When viewers were questioned about the performance it became evident that the minor detail of the notes had indeed been instrumental in this process, though at a quite unconscious level. The audience to whom the notes were visible assumed that when not addressing the camera the speaker was in fact referring to them. Viewers who had not seen the notes interpreted the deviation of his gaze from the camera as being due to pensive deliberation. Each of these assumptions was a tacit, automatic reading of the performer's behaviour, and neither group of viewers was aware of its influence on their attitudes towards him. Yet the inferences observed with respect to his lecturing ability were clearly based on these assumptions, and it is highly probable that their attitudes to the content of his lecture were affected in consequence. (This assertion is made as a result of each of the experiments we shall report.)

Experiment 2: adding a background As indicated earlier in the chapter, a technique commonly used in the straightforward 'head and shoulders' delivery of information is the addition of a visual background. When a news reporter, for example, presents his material from the studio rather than from a more relevant location, background display may be provided either by means of a rear projection or a 'keying' process (see chapter 2). While setting the speaker in a context relevant to his subject, background images may in certain circumstances be usefully changed apace with the exposition. Even in cases where the image is not actually essential to the delivery (as with an abstract design or programme symbol), it is evidently supposed that the extra stimulation helps to maintain viewers' interest; and producers avoid a completely plain background at all costs.

In order to test the effects of visual background detail, a seventy-second news-type report of an archaeological dig by members of Liverpool University was prepared by a professional television newswriter. Two versions of the material were televised using two cameras immediately

Table 4.2

Experiment 2: Mean ratings of a TV presenter set against (+) a picture background and (o) a plain background

	1	2	3	4	5	6	7		t	$p<$
Unpleasant					o+			Pleasant	0·390	
Informed		o	+					Uninformed	0·671	
Strong			+	o				Weak	0·397	
Honest		+	o					Dishonest	2·134	0·025
Sceptical				o	+			Believing	1·082	
Shallow			o	+				Profound	2·228	0·025
Confusing					+	o		Straightforward	1·497	
Reliable			+	o				Unreliable	1·845	0·05
Direct			+	o				Evasive	1·190	
Interesting				o	+			Uninteresting	0·281	
Fair			+	o				Unfair	1·930	0·05
Expert				o	+			Inexpert	1·004	
Insincere					+	o		Sincere	0·557	

N.B. At $df = 23$, $t_{0·05} = 1·714$

89

adjacent. In one version the speaker was seen against a plain studio screen and in the other a landscape background relevant to his piece was combined with his image by an electronic 'keying' process. The two recordings were made simultaneously, and all characteristics relative to the speaker's performance (e.g. speed of delivery, vocal inflection, etc.) were thus invariant. The tapes were both shown to each of two student audiences numbering twelve and thirteen persons respectively and their assessments of the performance were obtained as in the previous experiment. As before, none of the subjects knew the performer.

An analysis of the responses is given in Table 4.2. It reveals that the speaker was not seen as more interesting when the keyed background was present: indeed the average rating of 'interest' in the keyed and non-keyed versions was statistically indistinguishable. (This observation conflicts with the general assumption on which the use of such techniques is based.) However, compelling effects in other directions were observed. When presented against the picture background, the speaker was construed as significantly more honest, more profound, more reliable, and more fair than when seen against the plain background. The keying process clearly had the effect of heightening his 'credibility' as a performer in this context and of increasing the amount of trust which viewers were prepared to invest in him. (It should be re-emphasised that in terms of the actual performance the two recordings were identical, and that the viewers' attitudes to it were thus influenced by the presence of the background context alone.)

On the other hand, experimental manipulation did nothing to distort the viewers' perceptions of the speaker's expertise as in the televised lecture situation reported in experiment 1. It may be that viewers attribute lesser expertise to a speaker in television reportage situations than in a lecture setting — realising, for example, that most news reporters generally work to someone else's script — although they are prepared to recognise his impartiality and objectivity. While the usual justification for visual background in terms of its contribution to a production's overall interest value is called into doubt by the experiment, the addition of a relevant background seems to have led, on balance, to a favourable increase in the speaker's perceived honesty. Other backgrounds might clearly be predicted to exert different effects (Baggaley and Duck, 1974; Canter, West and Wools, 1974).

Experiment 3: front view or profile? A further variable in the presentation of TV performers is the very angle at which they are seen. Even such an apparently neutral factor as this may be predicted to exert

Table 4.3

Experiment 3: Mean ratings of a TV presenter seen (+) addressing the camera and (o) in profile

	1	2	3	4	5	6	7	*t*	*p<*
Ruthless				+	- - o		Humane	1·05	
Fair			o -	- - +			Unfair	1·3	
Imprecise				+	- - o		Precise	0·69	
Expert				o -	- - -	- +	Inexpert	2·51	0·025
Partial		+o					Impartial	0·08	
Weak				+	o		Forceful	0·22	
Intolerant			+ -	- o			Tolerant	1·13	
Cautious					+o		Rash	0·09	
Unemotional				+ -	- - o		Emotional	1·29	
Intuitive				+o			Rational	0·21	
Relaxed			o -	- - +			Unrelaxed	1·06	
Direct		o - - +					Evasive	0·98	
Unreliable			+ -	- - o			Reliable	2·15	0·025
Sincere			o -	- - - - +			Insincere	1·37	

N.B. At $df = 15$, $t_{0.05} = 1·753$

unintentional effects on assessments of the performer's ability as indicated earlier in the chapter. To test this possibility, a one-minute address was televised on the subject of law and order. Two simultaneous recordings were made, presenting a head and shoulders view of the speaker from two angles. Seated against a curtain background, he addressed one camera directly and was shown by the other in half profile as though participating in a discussion (cf. Baggaley and Duck, 1975c). Focal length in the two recordings was identical, and in each the shot remained unchanged throughout the extract. Two student audiences, numbering eight and nine persons respectively, rated the performer, who was once again unknown to them. Their reactions to the two presentations were compared (Table 4.3) and assessments of the performer were indeed seen to be affected by the simple angle variation. Raban's (1975) contention, discussed above, that a direct to camera shot suggests greater impartiality than a half-profile shot, was not upheld. On several scales included specifically to test this prediction (partial/impartial, direct/evasive) no significant difference between the conditions was noted. However, in the half-profile condition, significantly higher ratings of the performer's reliability and expertise were obtained. And on all scales the half-profile condition drew more favourable ratings than the direct condition, even though the differences between them were not always statistically significant.

In popular usage the effects of camera angle on a performer's appearance have long been exploited — the low-angle shot, for example, making a small man (Alan Ladd) seem larger, and a big man bigger (cf. *Citizen Kane*). Producers know well that the qualities of a man's physical appearance suggest further characteristics which may be amplified or minimised by camera technique according to their purposes. Variations in camera height, therefore, are a ready source of bias in this respect, in view of the vast array of stereotypes already linking character and physical stature generally. A lateral variation between full-face and profile shots, however, had a coded significance which is less easy to decipher. At one level we may interpret this effect in terms of the obvious difficulties of addressing a TV camera as naturally as one would another person. On the other hand, it is possible that variables such as camera angle may exert effects in the context of particular conventions for camera usage. In news and general discussion contexts it is certainly traditional that those who address the camera directly are typically the reporters and linkmen, those who transmit the news rather than initiate it. The expert on the other hand is more often seen either in interview or in discussion, and thus in profile. Unless the speaker may be assumed an expert on some other basis — which, as observed in the previous experiment, the conventional

92

television reporter is not − the probability that he is expert and reliable in what he says will therefore be weighed as greater if he is seen in profile than if he addresses the camera directly.

In a different context, of course (using, for example, a different performer and text), the effects observed here might well be reversed, a direct to camera address suggesting greater directness of approach (and its attendant qualities of authority and impartiality) according to the prediction by Raban (1975). It is consistent with the contextual explanations that we advance for these effects, and should be re-emphasised, that our results should *not* be taken out of context as indicating rules for TV presentation in general.

Experiment 4: audience shots The first three experiments made plain the extent to which viewers' reactions to television material may be influenced by even the most subtle of presentation variables. When viewed in the relatively impoverished context of a solo 'head and shoulders' delivery, a TV performer may be assessed in terms of simultaneous visual cues which at face value appear quite marginal. In a discussion context, further cues to a speaker's ability may derive from shots showing the reactions to him of others (cf. Duck and Baggaley, 1974a, b): even when such reaction shots are not an essential part of the discourse, they are frequently presented for the simple purpose of increasing a production's interest value, though our findings so far indicate that they may have unintentional effects also.

The subtlety of effects deriving from sequential shots has already been indicated by the pioneers of film analysis (see chapter 1). In the fourth experiment different shots were juxtaposed in sequence to determine whether those of a lecture audience, for instance, may indeed affect the general interest value of the presentation alone, or are liable to have entirely unintended biasing effects in other directions. Two basic videotapes were prepared, each featuring the same sequence from a lecture on welfare economics. The sequence lasted three and a half minutes and was made with a single camera at a fixed distance from the lecturer. At the same points in each recording, shots of an audience were inserted, prepared independently with the help of a group of student actors and edited into the lecture to give the illusion that audience and lecturer had been together at the time of recording. On one tape, members of the audience were shown looking interested, attentive, stimulated and impressed ('positive' reactions), and on the other tape they appeared bored, inattentive and unimpressed ('negative'). Care was taken in editing to ensure that the length of audience shots and the points at which they

Table 4.4

Experiment 4: Mean ratings of a TV lecturer given (+) positive and (o) negative audience reactions

	1	2	3	4	5	6	7		t	p<
Confusing	o	---------	+					Straightforward	2·740	0·01
Strong				+	- - - o			Weak	1·001	
Honest		o	- +					Dishonest	0·626	
Shallow			o	- - - -	+			Profound	2·001	0·05
Ruthless				o	- +			Humane	0·479	
Insignificant			o	- - - -	+			Important	1·489	
Reliable			+ o					Unreliable	0·071	
Interesting				+	- - - - - - - -	o		Uninteresting	2·771	0·01
Popular				+	- - - - - - - - - - -	o		Unpopular	4·350	0·001
Nervous			o - - +					Not nervous	0·841	
Fair				+ o				Unfair	0·246	
Humorous					+ o			Not humorous	0·062	
Expert			+	- - - - - -	o			Inexpert	1·927	0·05
Inferior			o	- - +				Superior	1·005	
Unpleasant					o +			Pleasant	0·569	
Sincere		o +						Insincere	0·127	

N.B. At $df = 23$, $t_{0·05} = 1·714$

94

were inserted in the recording of the lecture were identical in both tapes. The prediction that judgements of the lecturer would be influenced by the types of audience activity shown was then tested on two groups of students, comprising twelve and thirteen persons respectively, in the usual manner. As in the other experiments, none of the subjects knew the performer.

The insertion of audience reaction shots exerted particularly powerful effects upon the perceived interest value and popularity of the performer as predicted. These are shown in Table 4.4. These results indicate the immense illusory power of the editing process generally and the clear propagandist uses to which it can be put. By far the most significant finding in this respect is that in the negative tape the lecturer was seen as more confusing, more shallow and more inexpert. As before, it is important to remember that the lecture performance itself and its contents were absolutely identical in the two tapes and that these effects cannot therefore be due to any activity on the lecturer's part. They are due solely to the inclusion of the audience shots in the final presentation.

Experiment 5: interviewer shots   Taking the evidence regarding reaction shots and editing effects together, we may predict that the editing technique commonly used to fake an interaction between two people, as we have described in chapter 2, may lead to an immense range of unintended effects upon audience reactions to both performers and to the discussion as a whole. Accordingly, an experiment was conducted with two purposes: (1) to test whether the reaction shots faked by an interviewer in the recording of edited 'cutaway' shots may disrupt the audience's assessments of him; and (2) to assess the differential effects of these 'simulated reactions' upon assessments of the respondent.

An extended interview was televised using a plain studio setting and two participants who faced each other in easy chairs. Both participants were well-known to one another, and an easy, spontaneous discussion ensued in which the interviewer, a lecturer in English Literature with acting experience, questioned the respondent on his latest book of poetry. Two cameras were used, one giving a fixed shot of the interviewer and the other a varying shot of the respondent. The videotape recording was directed *extempore*, giving maximum coverage to the respondent and occasional shots of the interviewer asking questions and reacting to the replies. As the discussion developed, each question was noted by a stenographer; and when it was over the interviewer was asked to repeat certain questions as naturally as possible – even though deprived of the interactive feedback normally available from the respondent – and to give a few standard reactions for subsequent editing purposes. (At no stage did the interviewer know the purpose of the experiment; and he assumed the latter procedure to be routine studio practice. As an actor he was able to perform the task of 'faking' interactive behaviour with evident ease.)

The introduction and early part of the interview was isolated, lasting three and a half minutes. Two versions of it were prepared: in one the straight two-camera version of the discussion was presented, and in the other the interviewer shots were replaced by the *post hoc* cutaways. The shots of the respondent were identical in both versions; and care was taken to ensure that the continuity and natural quality of the apparent interaction in the edited version was as far as possible preserved.

The analysis of this experiment is more extensive than that of the previous four, for the tapes were shown firstly to two student audiences (numbering twelve and thirteen persons respectively) for ratings of the interviewer, and secondly to a further two student audiences (both comprising ten persons) for ratings of the respondent. None of the subjects knew either participant. In the edited version, the *interviewer* was seen as significantly more tense than in the natural version (Table 4.5), despite his actor's ability to behave naturally in a highly artificial situation. Interestingly, however, he was also rated as significantly more sincere and more straightforward in this situation. (It would appear that the apparent conviction and clarity of his performance were improved despite his perceived strain in giving it.) On this occasion at least, the careful use of editing facilities was thus seen on balance to have had a beneficial influence on audience reactions; though when the one camera cutaway technique is used less carefully, and the interviewer is less adept at simulating the appropriate responses, less desirable effects might equally be predicted. When accompanied by less favourable performance traits than observed here, an increase in a performer's perceived tension alone would certainly have a detrimental effect on his psychological impact.

Analysis of audience reactions to the *respondent* in the two videotape versions revealed significant differences on a surprisingly large number of scales (Table 4.6). In the edited version he was seen as significantly more reliable and fair, more humane and more pleasant — without exception, his perceived qualities were enhanced by the editing procedure, even though the only shots varied were those of the interviewer. In addition to making these general character assessments, the audience rated him as significantly less confusing, more profound, and more expert — all effects pertaining to his actual intellectual credibility. It should be noted of course — in relation to each of the experiments — that, if the audience is

Table 4.5

Experiment 5a: Mean ratings of a TV interviewer seen (+) in actual interaction and (o) in simulated interaction with the respondent

	1	2	3	4	5	6	7		t	$p<$
Sincere				o - - - +				Insincere	2·194	0·025
Pleasant			+ - - - o					Unpleasant	1·195	
Honest				o - - - +				Dishonest	1·206	
Shallow			+ - - o					Profound	0·919	
Tense		o - - - - - +						Relaxed	2·738	0·01
Ruthless					o+			Humane	0·171	
Believing				o - +				Sceptical	0·537	
Hostile						o - - - +		Friendly	0·963	
Inferior				o - +				Superior	0·126	
Reliable				o - - +				Unreliable	1·009	
Direct					o - - - - - +			Evasive	1·221	
Straightforward					o - - - - - +			Confusing	2·090	0·025
Expert		o - - +						Inexpert	0·249	
Nervous			o +					Not nervous	0·863	
Fair			o +					Unfair	0·561	
Stable					o+			Unstable	0·258	

N.B. At $df = 23$, $t_{0·05} = 1·714$

Table 4.6

Experiment 5b: Mean ratings of a TV respondent seen (+) in actual interaction and (o) in simulated interaction with the interviewer

	1	2	3	4	5	6	7		t	$p<$
Confusing				+	o			Straightforward	1·955	0·05
Strong					o	+		Weak	1·800	0·05
Honest		o	+					Dishonest	1·253	
Shallow				+	o			Profound	2·595	0·01
Ruthless					+	o		Humane	3·161	0·005
Insignificant		+	o					Important	1·069	
Reliable			o	+				Unreliable	2·378	0·025
Interesting				o	+			Uninteresting	1·647	
Popular				o+				Unpopular	0·195	
Nervous			o +					Not nervous	0·241	
Fair		o		+				Unfair	2·639	0·01
Humorous					o	+		Unhumorous	0·691	
Expert			o	+				Inexpert	2·086	0·05
Inferior			+ o					Superior	0·629	
Unpleasant				+		o		Pleasant	3·422	0·005
Sincere		o	+			o		Insincere	0·958	

N.B. At $df = 18$, $t_{0.05} = 1.734$

already familiar with the lecturer or his content, such effects may not occur; they are predicted solely in circumstances of ambiguity. Nonetheless, in this last experiment, the strength of the effects is most marked.

Combined effects of image variation

The previous five experiments have indicated a range of individual presentation variables influencing audience reactions to the credibility of TV performers as well as to their general interest value. However, in normal TV context presentation techniques are to be observed in constant interaction with each other, not singled out as we have carefully done in the preparation of the experimental material reported. Thus the significance of the effects so far isolated is constrained by the very fact of their isolation. Moreover, using a different performer, situation and text there is no *prima facie* reason why the effects should ever be repeated. Accordingly a sixth experiment was designed, permitting us to test simultaneously the hypotheses drawn from our earlier series in a combined format.

The interpretations of the previous experiments are recalled in Table 4.7. In each case the experimental manipulation was regarded as adding

Table 4.7

Interpretation of experiments 1–5

Experimental manipulation	Effects interpreted as due to
(1) Notes/no notes	Marginal context
(2) Background detail	Relevant context
(3) Direct/profile	Eye contact factors/ conventional use of camera
(4) Audience shots	Social approval cues
(5a) Interviewer shots	(Different performance)
(5b) Interviewer shots	Social approval cues

contextual detail related to the performer's reportive or discussive credibility. In experiment 6, the types of effect identified in isolation were combined in a two-way multivariate design.

A five-minute piece of videotape material was prepared with the chosen format of an appeal (a charity — the British Vagrancy Trust — was invented for the purpose). 'Peter Lewis', director of the BVT, was depicted in a studio scene requesting urgent funds to aid the construction of new vagrancy advisory centres and soup kitchens throughout the country. One basic performance was recorded by two cameras simultaneously (for the comparison of direct and profile shots appropriate to a reportive and discussive situation respectively), and three videotape copies of each version were made. In the second and third copies of each, additional levels of contextual detail were created by the edited insertion of supporting cutaway shots (Table 4.8). In all, six different visual

Table 4.8

Experiment 6: 'British Vagrancy Trust' appeal (six versions)

Format	Levels of contextual detail		
	(1) Unrelieved single shot	(2) Level (1) plus detail re performer	(3) Level (2) plus detail re message
Report (direct)	A	B (Cutaway showing notes)	C (Illustrative location shots)
Discussion (profile)	D	E (Cutaway showing interviewer reactions)	F (Illustrative location shots as in C)

presentations of the performance were thus produced. In each of them — reportive and discussive equally — the recorded performance was convincingly natural, for although he read his script from an autocue device as in experiment 3, the actor took care to hesitate over his words and look away from the camera occasionally as though delivering the material spontaneously.

Six separate groups of ten student subjects, none of whom had seen the actor previously, each viewed one of the six presentations. As in the previous experiments, their reactions to the performer were ascertained via semantic differential scales (Table 4.9); and the data were analysed for significant differences in the ratings across the six conditions. Although the actual spoken content of the appeal and the speaker's performance were identical in all conditions, certain assessments were indeed found to vary significantly according to the visual treatment. Table 4.10 gives the results of a two-way analysis of variances between the questionnaire scales

Table 4.9

Experiment 6: semantic differential scales

Tense	Relaxed
Strong	Weak
Persuasive	Unpersuasive
Ruthless	Humane
Unpleasant	Pleasant
Spontaneous	Rehearsed
Confusing	Straightforward
Friendly	Unfriendly
Shallow	Profound
Uninteresting	Interesting
Popular	Unpopular
Inexpert	Expert
Honest	Dishonest
Reliable	Unreliable
Unfair	Fair
Sincere	Insincere

Table 4.10

Experiment 6: comparison of versions by ANOVA/2

Source	SS	df	ms	F	p
A	875·665	15	58·377	25·108	$< \cdot 001$
B	69·117	5	13·823	5·945	$< \cdot 01$
A × B	176·166	75	2·348	1·010	ns
Error	2009·300	864	2·325		

A = questionnaire scales
B = visual treatments

101

as one factor and the visual treatments as the other. The visual condition which this analysis shows to have been significantly the *least* acceptable was that in which the direct presentation to camera was combined with cutaway shots showing notes (*C*). The *most* acceptable condition was that in which profile shots were presented in combination with interviewer reaction shots and location detail (*F*). Each of these results supports findings in the previous experiments and suggests that the effects of the contextual cues we have investigated may indeed be relatively constant, even though the subject matter of presentations is different.

As to the particular scales on which these preferences are indicated, the greatest effects were observed on the expert/inexpert dimension (Fig. 4.1), reaffirming the effects of visual presentation on performers'

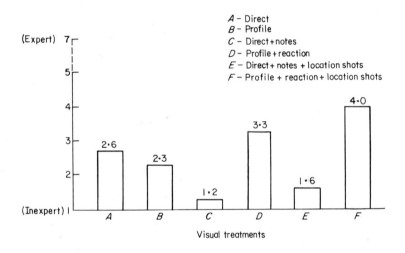

Fig. 4.1   Experiment 6: expert/inexpert dimension

expertise observed previously. Of course an immense number of comparisons between the various conditions are possible using these data; and the comparison of combined conditions *A/C/E* and *B/D/F* demonstrates that the effects of the direct/profile variable are particularly marked on the judgements of expertise specifically. Even though the previous direct/profile finding is replicated in the present experiment, however, we still remain cautious as to its predictability in TV contexts generally; and we have accordingly restricted our analyses to a comparison of the reactions on each scale across the six presentation conditions.

102

A second set of ratings significantly affected by the visual treatments were those in which the performer was judged as straightforward/confusing (Fig. 4.2). In common with the effects observed on the

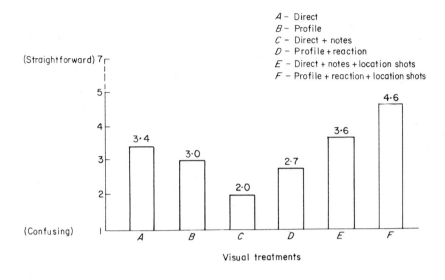

Fig. 4.2   Experiment 6: straightforward/confusing dimension

expert/inexpert scale, the least favourable presentation on this scale (i.e. the most confusing to subjects) was again that combining direct shots with detail of notes (C), and the most straightforward was that combining profile and reaction and location shots (F).

The same pattern is observed in the significantly differentiated reactions to the relaxation/tension of the performer (Fig. 4.3), in which the perception of the speaker as more tense in the direct conditions combining notes (C and E) combines with a tendency – albeit non-significant – to view these performances as more rehearsed. In this light the effect may relate to the realisation by modern viewers, already discussed, that television performers in the formal 'direct to camera' situation generally perform to a strict script, rehearsal and time schedule.

Although the direct plus notes condition (C) has clearly emerged from these analyses as the least preferred condition, it is interesting to note the significantly perceived 'strength' of the performer in this condition (Fig. 4.4). The suggestion that presentation variables may lead to significant though psychologically conflicting judgements of a performer

103

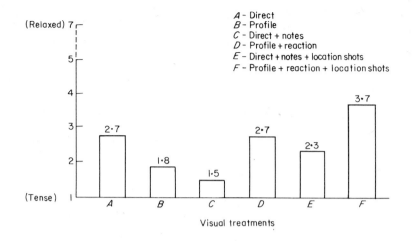

Fig. 4.3   Experiment 6: relaxed/tense dimension

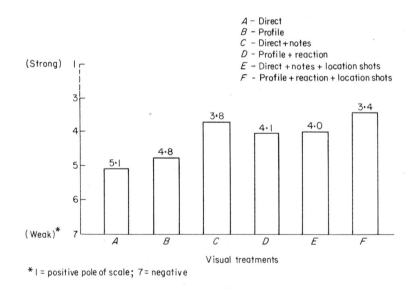

Fig. 4.4   Experiment 6: strong/weak dimension

104

simultaneously recalls Festinger's (1957) concept of 'cognitive dissonance': the use of presentation techniques to create dissonant attitudes in an individual certainly requires examination in view of the insidious persuasive effects they might have.

If we were to draw further conclusions at this stage, however, we would certainly risk running beyond the bounds our actual data describe. In the final section of this chapter we therefore summarise the main conclusions to which our investigations to date have led us, with particular respect to the power and diversity of presentation effects in TV contexts generally.

Experimental conclusions

The six experiments described above offer convincing support for the case presented in the earlier chapters — that the simple visual imagery of a television production may actually dominate its verbal content, overriding audience reactions to it in several ways. It appears that in ambiguous situations viewers use presentation cues in deciding whether the performer is worth listening to, and that attention to his spoken content may follow as a secondary process. From each of the above analyses it is also clear that the impact of any particular manipulation in visual presentation may bear no relation to the importance which could have been attached to it intuitively. Minor contextual sources of information about a speaker (such as those provided in experiments 1 to 3) can have the same types of effect on audiences' judgements as those created by the major types of cue provided by the reactions of others (as in experiments 4 and 5). In the absence of the latter more compelling types of information, viewers may become even more inventive in their reactions to tenuous and superficial contextual cues than usual. In no human confrontation imaginable are we prepared to accept unquestioningly another's statements without some indication of his right to make them and of his good faith, and on television it is thus only to be expected that the first impression a person makes will be determined not only by him but also by those who present him and by the visual imagery of the medium itself.

The effects of the physical image of a performer upon the conceptual image the audience has of him may actually derive either from the visual types of context we have emphasised, or from a form of non-visual context such as that of the conventional stylistics for camera usage perceived over time (cf. experiment 3). The finding recurrent throughout these experiments that presentation techniques may be used in order to heighten not only the interest value of a production but also the evident credibility and expertise of the programme presenter indicates that the effects of presentation are not only stronger than previously supposed, but also more varied. The use of television according to the criterion of visual interest alone evidently exploits only one of its dynamic properties. A criterion of credibility is in evidence which TV producers may consider in developing new techniques for their medium's use in different contexts. The practical and ethical implications of this observation are considered here in the remaining chapters.

Of course, the range of possible presentation effects is infinite, and their likely combinations are as varied and dynamic as the creative skills of those who produce them. Moreover, with the constant development of new television conventions (cf. chapter 2) the effects will be subject to dynamic modification. (As the facilities for a discussion over video-link develop, for instance, the effect produced by the direct/profile manipulation (experiment 3) may certainly diminish as more participants at all levels of expertise are seen to address the camera directly than was once the case.) It is thus imperative that our results should be regarded as specific to the very restricted types of context we have investigated in these experiments, and we re-emphasise that the effects we have reported are unlikely to derive in situations where the audience is familiar with the performer on more reliable bases. It is in the initial, short term stages of a viewer's reaction to a performer that such effects are likely to operate most strongly. As more reliable information about him accumulates, the reactions to a specific performer based on cues such as this are likely to be outweighed, though the dynamic power of television to exert such effects at all is nonetheless exceedingly important in the analysis of its general impact. As Potter (1975) indicates, the covert means by which one may be induced to place faith in the content mediated by television are — especially if deliberate — readily comparable with those of subliminal advertising:

> The peculiar danger of television as a medium lies in the intensity of its impact. This comes from the vividness of the picture, which is an immeasurably more powerful vehicle than words. All television is subliminal advertising . . . the viewer is continually registering in his mind situations which he may not realise that he has seen: women always in kitchens, coloured men always outsiders. (p.17)

It is to the persuasive dynamics of television in general terms that we turn in the next chapter.

References

Argyle, M. (1969), *Social Interaction*, London, Methuen.

Argyle, M. (1975), *Bodily Communication,* London, University Paperbacks.

Argyle, M. and Kendon, A. (1967), 'The experimental analysis of social performance', in Berkowitz, L. (ed.), *Advances in Experimental Social Psychology*, vol. 3, New York, Academic Press.

Aronson, E. and Carlsmith, J. M. (1968), 'Experimentation in social psychology', in Lindzey, G. and Aronson, E. (eds), *Handbook of Social Psychology*, vol. 2, Reading, Mass., Addison-Wesley.

Baggaley, J. P. and Duck, S. W. (1974), 'Experiments in ETV: effects of adding background', *Educational Broadcasting International*, vol. 7, no. 4.

Baggaley, J. P. and Duck, S. W. (1975b), 'Experiments in ETV: effects of edited cutaways', *Educational Broadcasting International*, vol. 8, no. 1.

Baggaley, J. P. and Duck, S. W. (1975c), 'Psychological effects of image variations', *Video and Film Communication,* March.

Baggaley, J. P. and Duck, S. W. (1975d), 'Experiments in ETV: further effects of camera angle', *Educational Broadcasting International*, vol. 8, no. 4.

Canter, D., West, S. and Wools, R. (1974), 'Judgements of people and their rooms', *Brit. J. Soc. Clin. Psychol.*, vol. 13.

Duck, S. W. and Baggaley, J. P. (1974a), 'Persuasive Polish', *New Society*, 18 July.

Duck, S. W. and Baggaley, J. P. (1974b), 'ETV production methods vs educational intention', *Educational Broadcasting International*, vol. 7, no. 3.

Duck, S. W. and Baggaley, J. P. (1975b), 'Experiments in ETV: interviews and edited structure', *Educational Broadcasting International*, vol. 8, no. 2.

Duck, S. W. and Baggaley, J. P. (1975c), 'Experiments in ETV: effects of camera angle', *Educational Broadcasting International*, vol. 8, no. 3.

Festinger, L. (1957), *A Theory of Cognitive Dissonance*, New York, Harper and Row.

Goodhardt, G. J., Ehrenberg, A. S. C. and Collins, M. A. (1975), *The Television Audience: Patterns of Viewing*, Farnborough, Saxon House.

Howitt, D. and Cumberbatch, G. (1975), *Mass Media Violence and Society*, London, Paul Elek.

Kelley, H. H. and Woodruff, C. L. (1956), 'Members' reactions to apparent group approval of a counter-norm communication', *J. Abn. Soc. Psychol.*, vol. 52.

Lyons, J. (1972), 'Human Language', in Hinde, R. A. (ed.), *Non-Verbal Communication*, Cambridge, Cambridge University Press.

Osgood, C. W., Suci, G. and Tannenbaum, P. (1967), *The Measurement of Meaning*, Chicago, University of Illinois Press.

Potter, J. (1975), 'ITV: critics and viewers', *Independent Broadcasting*, 4.

Raban, J. (1975), Review, *Radio Times*, 7 November.

Scheff, T. J. (1973), 'Intersubjectivity and emotion', *American Behavioral Scientist*, vol. 16.

Warr, P. and Knapper, C. (1968), *The Perception of People and Events*, London, Wiley.

Williams, E. (1974), 'An analysis of gaze in schizophrenics', *Brit. J. Soc. Clin. Psychol.*, vol. 13.

Williams, R. (1974), *Television: Technology and Cultural Form*, London, Fontana.

5   Television and persuasion

In a sense the results of the experiments in the previous chapter speak for themselves: they show a range of usually unintended influences on the viewer that are produced by commonly used presentation techniques. As such they support our introductory argument: that individuals have certain needs when perceiving anything and rely on available cues to satisfy them. This argument can also be applied to the perception of programme material that aims and intends to *persuade* as well as that which serves a simple *informative* function. Persuasive material on television, as we shall see here, makes use of certain types of cues through which the viewer may be led to certain inferences about the object of the persuasion. Thus advertising techniques contain cues about the credibility of the advertiser; political and propogandist broadcasts contain cues leading to enhancement of the speaker's image, and propaganda contains structural, contextual and direct cues that lead to more willing acceptance of the propagator's message. Our proposition in this chapter, then, is that the techniques used in persuasive TV material contain the same sorts of elements as those that we have identified earlier in the book, even though our work in that connection refers to educative or informative material specifically. The analysis therefore raises the question of parallels between the processes of persuasion on the one hand and information-giving on the other, whilst also asking whether the separation between them is always as clear as is often believed. (Let it be clear that we are not saying that informative programmes set out deliberately to persuade or mislead: we say simply that the dichotomy between the two programme types is not as clear as it may seem at first sight, and that there is further need to distinguish between both intentional *and* unintentional influence, not just at the level of editorial selection, but also at the level of production design.)

It can thus be seen that there are also certain implications of our previous results which do *not* speak for themselves. Indeed, the results themselves raise a number of complex issues, both in connection with their relationship to other influences of TV upon the viewer and at the level that explains why individuals respond to the cues inherent in production techniques at all. Both of these problems can be illuminated by consideration of the function of TV in relation to viewers' *needs* for structure and information, which leads ultimately to an examination of the role of TV in the social context as a source of information and ideas generally. The implications of our previous discussions of the viewing experience will henceforward be considered specifically. We seek to examine the needs which TV creates in the viewer or which it manipulates or subserves for them. Thus we seek not only to take the argument into new areas that have not been discussed here previously but also to suggest a relationship between our experimental findings and the traditional field. For the effects reported in the previous chapter could clearly be used to enhance the credibility of performers whether or not their intended function is socially acceptable, and at some point one will be faced squarely with a decision about whether some of these uses infringe ethical standards.

Viewers' needs and social context

Two features combine to increase modern man's reliance on TV as a general information source: his need for hypothesis allied to structure (cf. chapter 3); and the increasing complexity and technological diversification of modern commerce and daily life. The former of these features predisposes him to rely on others for guidance, and the latter both increases the need for guidance and restricts the outlets from which it may usefully be obtained. The days are long since past when an individual could, for example, either tell for himself the difference between the various clothing fibres offered to him or ask a friend to do it for him (Glasser, 1967), when no choices were involved between the different claims of the different makes of transport (they were all horses), and so on. Hence the days are long since past when an individual could reasonably expect to carry in his head all the information that he needed for making rational and measured decisions in carrying out his daily enterprises – or when he could simply consult other members of his close community for the appropriate advice. Modern technology is now so complex that individuals do not expect to understand even the general principles of some of the things that they employ daily (e.g. telephones, cassette recorders, television itself, electricity). To that extent, the former, presumably reliable, sources of information are easily replaced by a more accessible and wide ranging source which has faster access to 'experts', namely television. This now exerts a much more urgent influence on viewers' motives and needs than ever the previous social context provided (cf. Peterson, Jensen and Rivers, 1965). For this reason it has become the means through which it has been assumed that man's other needs can be manipulated, accentuated and channelled. Such effects, as we have seen in chapter 4, may be either intentional or unintentional.

The need to order and understand his environment is a basic requirement for every individual (Kelvin, 1970), and his reliance on other people for the data by which he comes to understand the world, to evaluate his own abilities, and to assess others' attitudes towards him is indicated by Festinger (1954; cf. also chapter 3). Indeed, an exceptionally effective way of breaking down resistance to persuasion (or to its extreme form: brainwashing) is to provide the individual with as little evidence as possible about how *others* are reacting. In Korea this was effected by the Chinese Communists' practice of placing individuals in strange or alien groups, by breaking down the structure of existing groups, by dividing members of groups against one another through competition for food and resources, by encouraging informing against others, and by bestowing special privileges as rewards for disloyalty to others (Lifton, 1961). On the other hand, an effective way of actually changing an individual's attitudes is to give him plenty of evidence about how other people behave in similar circumstances — particularly if that helps him to follow them to the goal that is desired by the changing agent. A blatant example of this effect is provided by advertisements which attempt to create the impression that other people who are, in most other respects, similar to the viewer are actually getting more out of life than he is because they use a particular product.

The psychological effects of television as an advertising agent evidently derive in the following way. For one thing an individual belongs simultaneously to several groups and for another, an individual's search for reference points can be satisfied by television's presentation to him of evidence about how other people behave; the context in which TV is viewed (i.e. in the privacy of one's own home in the presence of very few other individuals) also emphasises this function of TV by removing the viewer from contact with a larger reference group, and raises dependence on the cues inherent in the programme content and context. (It constitutes a reduced social environment in which to receive information, and thus deprives the individual of direct knowledge of the responses of others to that information.) In the latter connection we should realise that the loneliness of the long distance TV viewer separates him from the very reactions of groups of others which *are* present when he views a cinema film, for example, or — as in bygone days — a cinematic newsreel. In relation to television's particular impact in the home, we should note the observation by Packard (1964) that in the soothing and familiar environment of one's own household the ready acceptance of persuasive and informative material is much increased (hence the importance for a door to door salesman of an attempt to gain access to the home). These points tie in closely with the previous arguments and point to the natural reliance of viewers on, for example, the social interaction cues provided by production techniques, given the impoverished social environment in which the programmes are viewed. We shall therefore now examine the rationale for television's persuasive impact within a given social context in more detail. We are specifically concerned here with *generally* observable social needs which all men have, and the ways in which TV serves them. We are thus not concerned here with the needs which TV actually creates (see below) but with those which stem from man's humanity and from the social processes bearing upon it.

The error in regarding any communication process (and thus the dynamics of television) as having no relationship to the individual's situation in a social context or to his position in and interaction with other social groups has been pointed out by Secord and Backman (1974). Individuals do not watch TV after adopting fundamentally different psychological processes from those used in everyday life — they do not suddenly become stimulus sponges with no interpretative skills; they do not lose the processes of hypothesis that characterise their everyday lives in other spheres; nor do they become psychologically isolated from the influence of the groups to which they belong. Consequently, it is quite false to see communication simply as

> ... a process that occurs between a single communication source and a single recipient ... Research has made it abundantly clear that the effects of a communication depend upon the respective places of the communicator and the respondent in the structure of society and upon their immediate relations to other persons and groups. (Secord and Backman, 1974, pp.128–9)

In other words, the impact of a communication upon an individual is modified by the influence of the groups to which the individual belongs, by his relationships with other members of the group — and by their reactions to the communication.

These authors go on to show ways in which research on group decisionmaking has emphasised the difference between individuals' responses to persuasive material in lectures (where the recipient is, they say, passive) and in groups (where the recipient is evidently an active member). Clearly, in the context of our present discussion, the process of watching TV has more similarities to the process of watching a lecture than to the process of active participation in group discussion. However, once this point is made, and once it is recognised that the simple view of communication ('source addresses individual recipient') is naïve, it is also necessary to add that, in relation to viewers' actual responses to television, the Secord and Backman view is also inadequate in several ways. It is true that the individual recipient is a member of a group and a social context, but it is also true that he is *not* passive but active in his processing of incoming information, and that he actively seeks to structure and interpret it. He may certainly not be consciously active in his response to subtle cues such as those identified earlier (and consequently it becomes exceedingly difficult to show that even the most passively received 'information' is ever wholly free from some form of 'persuasion' and 'influence'). It is also true that membership of groups can be a two-edged weapon, both protecting the individual against persuasion and making him more vulnerable to it. As argued earlier, where the viewer has the chance to observe others' reactions, he can find some anchorage for his opinions about the material he sees. But because TV is habitually *not* viewed in this way, and because TV habitually sets out to portray to the viewer how others (are alleged to) behave, then TV can come to replace and suborn the normal protective influences of groups upon the individual by making it appear desirable that he should attempt to assess his behaviour by reference to other higher status or materially more satisfied groups. At first sight it appears that this occurs only through the influence of advertisements, but we will develop a position that argues this view to be naïve.

The bulk of our argument in this respect is set out later in this chapter, but the essential step has been made here in our statement that television encourages a dependence upon it in the manner by which it provides 'anchors for hypotheses' in an increasingly diversified world. Man's reliance on others and upon groups as reference points is replaced by a reliance on TV as the reference point, and by a view of the world that TV reflects through the content of its programmes. The dynamic of television, we have argued, takes considerable impetus from its influence on needs — particularly the need for information (which is why we suggest that information and persuasion are not so different as may be imagined). This is also the reason for our belief that the influence of the cues we have examined experimentally may be more significant than appears at first sight — by relating the two phenomena of persuasion and information with a bonding of 'conceptual glue'.

TV and need creation

We have concentrated so far on the ways in which TV provides the viewer with the opportunity to satisfy certain existing needs and in so doing we have looked mainly at the unintended influences which TV has upon the viewer. More commonly associated with its persuasiveness are the intended effects produced by TV, some obvious and some more subtle, and it is the junction between the intentional and unintentional that is our ultimate concern in this chapter: that point where the emphasis on placing TV at the service of the viewer shifts to one in which the viewer is placed at the service of TV and those who use it. The fact that viewers do have certain needs is, of course, clearly recognised in both the content and structure of TV programmes: what must be explained is the direction in which these needs are channelled and restructured because of the influence of TV specifically.

As a starting point for what follows, consider the simple, subtle, but significant influence of the mere presence of a television set as an item of furniture in the household (Glasser, 1967) – an influence on the very way that people structure their personal environment. Living rooms are now designed on a principle intended to give clear sightlines to the TV set itself: central ceiling lights have tended to be abandoned in favour of lower lighting levels from lower placed lighting sources; individuals sit side by side facing the TV set rather than opposite each other around a fireside. Even when not overtly persuasive, TV can affect the viewer in other ways. There is considerable research evidence (discussed by Secord and Backman, 1974; Aronson, 1973; and briefly in our preface) that viewers' values in respect of crime and violence are affected by the media; that escapist material influences viewers' beliefs and intentions – and that TV can displace active recreational outlets or other informational sources such as books (Himmelweit, Oppenheim and Vince, 1958). All of these and other determinist effects (Peterson, Jensen and Rivers, 1965) are generally regarded as 'non-persuasive influences of TV' since they are presumed unintentional. However, our point is that such a view is misleading and incomplete, since, in the light of our reported experiments, it appears that such effects may arise from within the individual quite independently of any processes intentionally manipulated by the medium itself. Whatever their origin – whether internal to the viewer or external; intentional or unintentional; consciously or unconsciously active – the dynamic effects of TV may be nonetheless completely influential. Placed in this pyschodynamic context, the distinction between intentional persuasion on the one hand and simple communication on the other is quite eclipsed. The effects which, therefore, concern us henceforward are those which, in the emphasis on intentional persuasion, have received less attention — indeed, have often been hived off for completely separate analysis — namely the effects of TV upon social and informational needs as well as its effect on material aspirations. It is an important part of our case that the effects noted above can all be seen to have derived from the same psychodynamic determinants of TV's influence: the satisfaction (through various types of cue) of the need for information, order and structure.

The basis of TV's persuasive impact in apparently neutral, informative contexts is thus the same as that of its effects in advertising advanced earlier. First, the medium tends to divorce the individual from primary contact with his reference groups, particularly at the point where he is actually watching a programme and assimilating its content; second, it has become quite simply a major source of fact and information within society. (The very apparent neutrality of factual, non-commercial TV content — e.g. news — may even increase the viewers' susceptibility to the persuasive cues operating within it.) It is in this setting that the unintentional and intentional influences of TV on the viewer come together. Since the viewer is increasingly separated from his anchor points, his defences are lowered; since he looks to TV for information, he is more susceptible to the influence of the way it is actually presented and may derive some of his opinions from it consciously or unconsciously — especially where highly complex issues are involved and where the need for a credible information source is rendered more important to him. The argument regarding unconscious persuasive influences generally is all the more plausible when it is realised that there are well-established 'sleeper' effects observed in research on attitude change: that is, the influence of a communication upon attitudes is often not apparent until some considerable time after the communication itself has actually been *forgotten* (Aronson, 1973). In this context, it should be noted that the experiments reported in the previous chapter may be interpreted as pointing to sleeper effects on viewers' perceptions of *sources* of information.

Reverting, then, to the point that opened this section: it appears that the direction in which TV channels and restructures viewers' needs is to raise the status of TV itself, to arrogate the role of a credible source of information and, as our analysis has it, to exert 'persuasive' influences on this basis. It has already been argued by others (e.g. Argyle, 1964) that frequent watching of TV tends to increase imitativeness and material ambition by the manipulation of viewers' needs and motives through advertising, and by the emphasis on certain sides of reality in plays and entertainment programmes. Our position is different from this in that we argue that TV's influence stems from its importance as a source of apparent 'fact' and from the very way in which it presents its images of 'reality'. Television's attempt to offer an unbiased coverage of reality was restated in the recent BBC Richard Dimbleby lecture (Wheldon, 1976), and the view was expressed that the job of TV news is to reflect reality ('what has happened'), while that of TV plays is to reflect a different sort of reality ('inward reality', 'inner experience'). We suggest, however, that this distinction is grossly overstated and that much of TV's dynamic stems from its role as a persuader, whether intentional or not. The statement by Wheldon is, of course, an expression of the supposition within journalism generally that bias can be avoided whenever required. To James Gordon Bennet (the American newspaper magnate) it appeared that newspapers should present 'news not views' and TV journalists (note the word) regard their product as broadly unbiased in this tradition so that even now it seems to most people that TV news programmes are sources of fact pure and simple. This, it should be noted, was also once held to be the status of advertisements – though, as Packard (1964) indicated, it is now quite clear that advertisers attempt to sell more than the simple product: they sell an image that goes with it, and they manipulate the image by means of cues which are powerful in their effects even though objectively they do not seem to amount to very much. As argued earlier in the book, TV is regarded as serving an entertainment function in particular, and, as a result of this, it has tended to aim in many of its programmes – even 'informative' news – for entertaining effects. As we have seen, the major justification for the use of TV's eye-catching effects in this respect stems from their presumed capacity to maintain viewers' interest (chapter 3). Evidently producers recognise the existence of certain needs in the viewer and set about the process of serving them by means of their technological skills. Whatever their reason, when faced with the task of informing viewers (e.g. in news programmes), producers make use of cues which serve an entertainment need superimposed on the informative purpose of the news broadcast and they do this (to echo the phrase used above) by means of cues which in themselves do not amount to very much. It is important to note in this context that the conventional TV journalist has an employment history largely based in newspaper journalism where there is early pressure to develop awareness that news is (quite literally) sold by the ability to captivate, amuse and entertain. In the development of TV journalism since the days when TV newsreaders were kept off the screen altogether, we have witnessed the replacement of a straightforward concentration on fact by a more popularist tabloid form of presentation. Whatever the production reasons behind this stylistic change, when dealing with simple informative requirements producers in the main make use of cues evidently serving an entertainment need and do so through cues whose effects are actually far subtler than is generally apparent.

It should be stressed that we do not imply any conspiracy here: we simply argue that the processes, skills and techniques used in presentation of informational programmes bear certain similarities to the overt aims and manipulative practices used in persuasive broadcasting. This of itself proves nothing: there are similarities between cows and horses, but there are also significant differences. However, since the techniques in both cases impinge on deep-rooted and all-pervasive psychological needs, their influence can be profound even when not intentional, and while the blatant use of subliminal advertising has been banned for this reason (and because of the manipulative intent of those who use it), the imperceptible and under-researched cues identified in our research do have parallel kinds of effect. At the obvious level, intentional bias can occur in the editorial selection of items for inclusion in news broadcasts (ranging from overt political bias in favour of one party to the more subtle bias conveyed by the selection of 'disastrous', 'critical', frightening, shocking or primarily 'bad' news); furthermore, just as unintended and unforeseen effects were produced by the introduction of TV sets to our homes, so too unintended, unforeseen and, we repeat, under-researched effects may be produced by use of the simple techniques identified earlier. For this and other reasons that become clearer later, we argue that even the apparently clinical and dispassionate TV news programme has a place in the discussion of TV persuasion and that the nature of its persuasive influence can be seen from the way in which televised persuasion works when intentional. We shall now therefore discuss the main features of advertising, political broadcasting, and general propaganda, and highlight similarities between the aims and intentions of such broadcasts and the purposes served by those programmes that inform intentionally and, perhaps, persuade unintentionally.

Persuasion and symbolism

The famous agent of Barnum and Bailey's Circus, R. F. Hamilton, once claimed that 'To state a fact in ordinary language is to permit a doubt concerning that statement'. As the power of this dictum has seeped through advertising agencies, the bombastic style of advertising has taken

..mple factual style that characterised the very earliest
.. Cynics may see parallels between this process and that
..lained of in the correspondence columns of *The Times:*
..ie over-use of extreme words like 'shock', 'disaster', 'crisis' and
. in reports of modern day events. These same cynics may note that
..rtisers subsequently abandoned bombast for the measured 'depth'
..pproach (manipulating hidden needs) and they may wonder whether
factual reporting will go the same way (e.g. by manipulating needs for
structure).

Advertisements do not create needs in people: they accentuate and
channel those that already exist, some of them at considerable depth
below the surface (Packard, 1964). They have thus tended to concentrate
less on the features or facts of the product itself than on promoting the
associations, symbolic correlates, or images of the product in people's
minds. In order to do this successfully and to evolve images which dredge
up recumbent needs and galvanise them into life, advertisers attempt to
understand the deep structure of behaviour, to accentuate petty
differences between their product and a competitor's, and to engender an
interest in the product by manipulating human ambitions (Glasser, 1967).
In doing this, they attempt to 'train' emotions, to direct attitudes and to
channel social behaviour patterns by means of techniques which operate
below the level of conscious thought.

It has been argued by Glasser (1967) that erosion of traditional
standards and traditional levels of knowledge has left the modern
individual with a diminished sense of direction. In relation to television we
may adapt this notion, suggesting that the ubiquitous presence of TV as
an 'expert' medium has compensated for this lack of direction, and has
encouraged a view of the world divorced from the individual's traditional
'social comparison' roots (cf. Festinger, 1954; and chapter 3). From his
claim that disorientation has occurred, Glasser goes on to argue that
advertisements, by seeming to offer direction (choices, opportunities), are
readily grasped by people wishing to orientate themselves. In other words,
deprived of the structure afforded him by satisfaction of certain needs,
the individual responds to cues which appear to offer some form of
concreteness or to narrow down the bewildering set of daily options with
which he is otherwise faced. Once this was recognised, Glasser argues, the
breakthrough for advertisers came when it was realised also that the most
powerful form of direction and concreteness stemmed from an
individual's own thought: in other words, when an individual's pre-exist-
ing psychological components could be built upon in order to persuade
him. For persuasion to be successful, the thoughts below the conscious

level need to be brought to the conscious level and encouraged to burgeon.

It is against this background that the claim has sometimes been advanced that buying something is a way of asserting one's own identity; or, more accurately, of stating what one would like one's identity to be. At this level, the advertiser ceases to sell a product and starts to sell a dream. The particularity of people's dreams lies in different directions, but eight general approaches have been developed by advertisers (Packard, 1964). These emphasise the needs for:

(1) *Emotional security* (provided by the suggestion, for example, that a product 'takes the worry out of life');
(2) *Reassurance of worth* (as offered by exalting the role of a drudge housewife);
(3) *Ego gratification* (observed in the attempt to make the consumer feel important in relation to the product and to other people);
(4) *Creative outlets* (suggested by hints that not all the work is done by the product: *'Together* you and Blanco can make a wonderful soufflé');
(5) *Love objects* (e.g., 'cuddly' children used to endorse baked beans);
(6) *Sense of power* (conveyed, for instance, by showing the product being used by people who take important decisions, or who drive powerful cars);
(7) *Sense of roots* (exploited by, for example, informing viewers that in the good old days, when people took care over their work, the viewers' grandfathers used to rely on the product); and,
(8) In the sale of some products only, a sense of *immortality and continued control* (e.g., the purchase of life assurance policies being represented as a means of exerting financial control over one's family after death).

There is also, of course, a strong sexual element inherent in many advertisements. All of the above examples serve to amplify the point that the simple message conveyed in any communication need be only one of the many 'meta-messages' that the recipient receives. It also emphasises that any responses need not be consciously directed, and that individuals need not necessarily be aware of either the influence process itself (since it is often so subtle) or of their own motivation that makes them susceptible to it. In summary, the style of advertisers' depth efforts is to look for the correct psychological knob to press in order to evoke from the recipient a direction of choice. We argue, in parallel, that, without looking for it, TV news presentation utilises one of these needs and operates with it unwittingly by providing cues for structure in its production techniques.

In TV presentation the motivations may be powerfully aroused by visual and auditory cues in combination, but in isolation the visual cues are generally thought to be more powerful than the auditory ones (Geertsma and Reivich, 1969). (Actually one would need to be cautious in generalising from this observation: for when the visual cues are ambiguous a soundtrack context can change interpretations of the visual image drastically. Shots of a young girl running through woods can take on a pastoral innocence or a chilling fearfulness simply according to the type of music accompanying them.) As in advertising, TV techniques in general serve strategically to present far more than the functional characteristics of the product: indeed they are expressly designed to manipulate the viewers' perception of the image and his attitude to the product accordingly. A popular advertising strategy, again using auditory cues, is to present a product using the voice of an actor who is, in another role, associated with particular qualities (of, for instance, strength and authority). The viewer is offered not simply the product alone but also symbolic reflections of the presenter. Since, in an informative or persuasive context, the most necessary characteristic for the viewer to perceive is *credibility* (chapter 4), it is this which presenters most consciously try to suggest. In TV news and current affairs programmes and advertisements alike, producers thus quite deliberately present far more than the basic hard facts. Indeed, TV news programmes often seem centred on the projection of an image of the presenter above all else. To use the advertising analogy, the viewer is offered not simply the news product alone but marketed symbols of the presenter's product worthiness.

Even if the cues to the audience interpretation of performers are not deliberately presented, it seems that viewers and other journalists will invent them. Since the TV newsreaders were first identified by name (chapter 1) they have become increasingly viewed, regardless of their own intentions, as 'TV personalities' (a curious phrase); the news value surrounding their actions and attitudes has escalated in the process. Recently a major and recurrent source of public interest has been BBC-TV's first woman TV newsreader, Angela Rippon. Although Miss Rippon has taken great professional care to present a neutral and depersonalised reading of the news, the public and journalistic attempt to categorise her in identifiable personality terms has led to a stereotyped depiction of her as 'cool', 'clinical' and 'aloof'. Try as performers might on TV to avoid a personality tag, it seems that labels will seek them out ultimately – even to the point where objective detachment is personified as 'cold aloofness'. Similarly the BBC-TV weather forecasters, plying their information in an equally business-like and unfussed fashion, attract press and audience ratings (and beratings) concerning their clothing and personal style − but no comment at all on their evident professional skills. 'He can spot an occluded front like none of the others' would be a comment suitably worthy of them − but their meteorological function in the viewers' eyes is given a secondary significance. Indeed, personal details most irrelevant to their professional role are drawn into the public arena despite their efforts. The private wedding of one BBC-TV weather forecaster once provided front page material for a *Daily Mail* 'exclusive' (19 February 1976): 'Barbara of the TV weather marries in secret'. The viewers' vested need to substantiate the image they perceive denies a TV performer any hope of being noticed for his basic qualifications − and, incidentally, denies the TV medium any chance of ever becoming fully transparent and neutral (unbiased) as, for the sake of its authoritative image particularly, it would dearly like to be seen.

In view of the richness of symbolic cues available to the viewer, let us therefore consider the ways in which symbols are consciously manu-factured. Soap advertisers have long recognised that their product should not be sold as something that increases cleanliness but rather as an aid to beauty or to social attractiveness. Similarly, toothpaste is not presented to the viewer of TV adverts as something that staves off disease and decay but as an agent of whiteness and sparkle. In other words, the function of the product is wrapped up by advertisers in a symbolic esoteric form that has greater appeal to the deeper and more self-acceptable needs of the viewer and potential consumer. But symbols are also subject to fashion. Whereas advertisements of the 'sixties tended to emphasise social and material aspiration, power and acquisition, events have recently created a spate of advertisements aimed at soothing viewers' fears about what the product does to the environment. Gleaming oil tankers are seen driving through unspoilt rolling moorland as the sun sets through a haze − clearly a symbolic reinforcement of claims that oil is something clean, fresh and natural − whilst earlier advertisements emphasised the contribution of oil to industrial production, and its powerful potential in car engines ('as used on the world's finest racing circuits').

Whilst this approach by advertisers contains its own particular drawbacks, and manifests clear and cogent parallels with the kind of effect noted in our experiments, it is the wider implications which concern us here − as they have concerned other writers who have devoted a greater part of their analysis to advertising methods. Glasser (1967) coined the phrase 'Ad-ucation' for the ways in which such advertising methods tend to educate viewers to expect a particular style of approach to any object, to condition them to superficialities, to lead them to be captivated by the witty pun or phrase at the expense of meaning. Ad-ucation also acts as a process whereby viewers adapt and habituate themselves to the standards and values of the advertisers, accepting the pressures to consume, purchase or cast off products that have 'obsolesced' through fashion change. In our terms, however, the ad-ucation process may not so much transmit values directly as provide the cues through which viewers can structure their experience in new ways — and news presentations contain similar cueing structures. Apart from those examined in depth in the previous chapter, news presentation attempts to 'market' the symbolic status of the presenter, accentuating his power, position or reliability rather than simply encouraging objective or detached analysis of his report; and it offers the viewer a series of clearly, symbolically identified experts to inform him on the detailed aspects of the news. Even the status of expert itself has thus become a symbol and is subject to the same manipulation as are other symbols in relation to the product that they symbolise. (Popular TV 'experts' in pure science fields are typically those presented with the symbolic trappings of a scientist: the rumpled shirt, the frenetic nervous movements. Television viewers (as the columnists Clive James and Alan Coren have both independently suggested) not only believe that all scientists *look* like mad scientists, they expect them to *behave* madly on television too and rate them accordingly: a successful TV scientist is thus one who confirms their prejudice.) In most scientific fields, however, expertise is indicated by complexity of knowledge, depth of information, the capacity to recognise different — even incompatible — explanations for the same phenomena, and the empirical testing of the theories that result. However, the twin needs of TV reporting (time pressure; and the need to 'entertain') often reduce opportunities for exposing the complexities of particular issues. Thus experts are invited to summarise or précis complex findings and problems for the sake of easier communication with an audience (and, indeed, with studio presenters) who have not the same familiarity with the problems, the usual approaches to them, or with their correct context, but desire simple information in a ready structure. Thus 'expertise' is often presented to the viewer as a smart answer to a simple question; and the myth of the 'seventies that, with a quick do-it-yourself guide, anyone can become an expert in any field from bricklaying to politics to conveyancing) gains and grows. Viewers are actually being misled in this respect in the same way as they are in advertisements.

Recognising the risks of this phenomenon, TV has often solved the problem by using a 'report' style where both sides of the case are presented in the studio, often by having interested members of the public in the audience to argue their side of the case. (The ultimate extension of this approach is found in 'access TV', discussed in the next chapter.) However it is superficial to assume that this is any more than an apologia. In such reports and discussions the essential background of expertise (time during which skills and knowledge are absorbed) is bound to be lacking; and the chance to put a complex case on television is further constrained by four main factors. First, TV demands a need for balance – notably in political broadcasting, but also, by extension, in any case where the viewer is encouraged to make up his own mind: this means that both sides of the argument must be exposed. However, the need for balance inevitably leads to the banal polarisation of the two sides into simplicities and the attempt to accentuate differences out of proportion to any similarities or common ground. The sight of one party attacking the other vigorously is more entertaining than the sight of two opponents compromising (unless, as sometimes happens, the programme has appointed itself arbitrator in the dispute). The need to entertain or to have entertainment components in a programme dictates either that especially popular issues get discussed or, where the subject matter is difficult, that the programme will contain glib and superficial 'demonstrations' of points, techniques, technology. Time constraints often mean that presenters, experts and contributors have to speak briefly, leaving out qualifications of their basic position, and that points are rarely pursued in the depth they require; this is often exacerbated during the very style of programme designed to produce greater balance, namely the audience participation programme where a large number of potential contributors fight for the opportunity to speak for a brief period. The tendency to mistake number for complexity is a part of all the above. The belief is that having as many people contribute as possible is the best way to ensure breadth of coverage of the issues. Ideally this would be so, but breadth and depth are orthogonal concepts and 'complexity' contains both.

There is a further consequence of the symbolic use of expertise which strengthens the parallels between the processes underlying informational programmes and advertisements. In serving its mediating function the TV report programme tends to focus on arguments about the content rather than on the content itself, since arguments are more entertaining than facts. A controversial Government Bill, information about joining the EEC, the case for giving up smoking, all have been presented to viewers in the form of arguments between opposing parties, usually preceded by a short film outlining 'the facts' – themselves chosen to make the ensuing discussion entertaining. Thus fifty pages of close print – which, for all their bureaucratic language, are usually a frank attempt to create something informed and unambiguous — are reduced to a symbolic presentation. The importance of this area of discussion becomes increasingly apparent at an organisational level of analysis. In the manipulation of opinions and attitudes by television we see a force by which governments are toppled and new ones created (government is founded on opinions, and opinions are manipulable). The systematic symbolisation of expertise, the concentration on argument in the absence of fact, the presentation of opinion as truth all accelerate the influence of TV on public opinion, and shape the dependence of viewers upon it. 'Facts' have become 'products' packaged just as in advertising; and in the process, techniques which have arisen in the commercial context have also infiltrated the televised presentation of non-commercial information. A marketing of opinions is thus created, and, where these bear on government, this becomes potentially sinister. Just as students of advertising have noted that advertisements not only suggest specific demands for their product but also purvey an attitude about consumers, fashion, material wealth or acquisition, so too the portrayal on TV of expertise, and the concentration on debate, conveys not only specific demands for a particular view of a given problem, but also an attitude about political or other issues, about what facts are, and about how experts go about their daily business. In similar vein, 'a scientist' on TV is presented as someone who finds out facts rather than one who tries to explain them by testing the predictive ability of different theories. 'A scientific expert' is thus a person with an encyclopaedic brain rather than a contemplative or arbitrative one, and his job is represented as being concerned with unearthing phenomena rather than explaining where they fit. Thus a statement by an expert is seen as a statement of the facts rather than an opinion or hypothesis about them, and viewers are led to believe that they are receiving information when they are actually receiving attitudes and opinions towards it. In a sense, it does not matter that this is the case as long as it is recognised as such. However, where real expertise in a complicated field is presented, and the expert is called upon to express the state of his art in summary form, the truth is that a full understanding of his opinions or his facts will require a lengthy training, such as the one he himself has had. When viewers are offered opinions as though they were facts, and are given the opportunity to make up their own minds about complex issues on the basis of evidence, the implication is that, as a general principle, no subject is beyond the grasp of an applied, if untrained, mind whose optic nerve is directed at a TV set or its associated publication. The marketing of this view is, in our opinion, as widespread and detrimental as is the influence by advertisements on people's attitudes to material wealth and acquisitions. News programmes, informational programmes and reports have, in our view, had a similar influence on viewers' attitudes to opinion and information.

Political broadcasting

Just as advertising is concerned with the creation of choice out of needs, so political and propagandist broadcasting is designed to create choice out of information and opinion. It is significant that most obvious forms of propaganda, as usually understood, are in evidence at times of maximum uncertainty (war, political upheaval) when anxiety is high and structure is low. It is also significant that definitions of propaganda have changed over the years from an emphasis on the selection of facts to an emphasis on opinions about facts, and thence to an emphasis on the manipulation of attitudes (below we shall consider the development in this direction of the influence exerted by TV on political debate).

The earliest use of the term 'propaganda' in anything like its modern form (although not the earliest example of the practice of propaganda) was during the Reformation, when Pope Gregory XV set up a body for the propagation of the faith (Sacra Congregatio de Propaganda Fide). Its brief was regarded as factual and educative, amongst other things to supervise the content of liturgical books. In 1923, Wreford defined propaganda as 'the dissemination of interested information and opinion', whilst Lasswell (1927) suggested that it was 'the management of collective attitudes by manipulation of the significant symbols'. Objecting that such definitions make it difficult to distinguish propaganda (in the negative sense) from education, Qualter (1968) places more emphasis on the intentions of the propagator, on his knowledge of whether he is disseminating truth or falsehood, and on the concentration of his work on attitudes rather than information pure and simple. He suggests that:

> Propaganda is . . . the deliberate attempt by some individual or group to form, control or alter the attitudes of other groups by the use of the instruments of communication, with the intention that in any given situation the reaction of those so influenced will be that desired by the propagandist. (p.27)

It is equally important, he argues, to understand both the means of communication available to the propagandist and also the fact that the propagandist uses a depth approach in attempting to influence particular groups. Similarities between this position and our own in the wider context of the influence of TV will be immediately apparent.

Other features of propaganda techniques act as a counterpoint to ideas we have already discussed. Propaganda tends to simplify complex issues and settle on striking or novel symbolic forms which will bear repetition. It tends to be concerned with personalities and images; it provides cues for structure; it attempts to generalise emotional attitudes from one situation to another. But more than anything, its meaning is gained from the way in which it presents material rather than from anything inherent in the material itself, and in this it makes deliberate use of whatever cues are available to serve its purpose. Whilst it is undoubtedly true that the motives of the propagandist are essential components in any decision about the status of propaganda — whether or not it is acceptable — it is the use of such methods for any reason, however innocent, that characterises much propaganda. Our point here is to draw parallels between the techniques used in such cases for conscious subversion and the unconscious uses of it in present forms of TV where no propagandist function is intended. The presentation principles are the same in both cases and ultimately the effect is the same, even if the intended purpose is different. The recognition of some of these similarities may serve to counteract the insidious effects of such techniques as discussed earlier, and it is important in this light to recognise that our analysis centres on the techniques by which information is conveyed (and on the cues that they contain) rather than on the information content more conventionally defined. We see propaganda as an attempt to manipulate attitudes about information in a complex and uncertain environment, and the attention-getting techniques employed in news and other informative programmes discussed earlier can be described as essentially such. Propaganda takes its power from the ability to manipulate attitudes by the way it presents the information and the images of those who report it.

The most obvious candidate for image building is the political candidate at election time. Of course the 'image' of a politician is electorally important to him at all times, and if he has no distinct personal projection he may find it difficult to advance towards the seats of power on the strength of his ideas alone. Once he has gained a position of authority he must ensure that the image he presents is publicly acceptable — and conducive to respect — as well as tolerable to his colleagues. In February 1975, Mrs Thatcher was elected the first woman leader of a British parliamentary party by her Conservative colleagues. Her need for a public image, previously indistinct, became paramount. Whether consciously on the part of her party machine, or unconsciously on the media's part as an attempt to create a tangible aura with which to associate her future deeds and sayings, the effort after image building was immediately undertaken. Film of Mrs Thatcher at the sink, Mrs Thatcher talking to men in the street, details of Mrs Thatcher as the daughter of a grocer: these became the staple fare of TV news and current affairs programmes for some weeks. To the purveyors of news (presumed hard and factual) the imagery software in which fact is couched was the primary source of concern.

The importance of television in modern politics cannot be, and nowhere is, disputed. As with that of advertising, the nature of its socio-psychological role must clearly be examined in two lights. For TV serves not only as a direct means of marketing particular political views (e.g. the views of particular parties) but succeeds also, through its concentration on attempts to 'analyse' political events (cf. the discussion of symbolic forms earlier) in marketing a general outlook, and in influencing viewers' attitudes to the very concept of political debate. Just as advertisers concentrate on distinguishing their product from virtually identical ones also on the market, so too the political parties tend to concentrate on accentuating differences between themselves and other parties, notwithstanding the oft-repeated view that 'all parties are the same'. In passing, it is interesting to note that this comment (containing as it does a slight hint of condemnation of politicians) is a complaint that arises from the very view that politicians have effectively produced in people's minds: namely that there are fundamental and significant differences between the parties on every single issue available for contemplation. These differences (or similarities) are transmitted via the medium of TV in various ways. The obvious means, the party political broadcast, has been available for many years, and in this connection the techniques often employed to accentuate differences and to market one's own views are broadly similar to those used directly by advertisers (careful selection of issues; concentration on the weak points of the competing 'products'; appeal to those individuals who are vacillating and who may possibly be subject to influence). Coupled with this are some of the other obvious and familiar techniques of persuasion discussed earlier in this book: order of presentation of material; rhetoric; authority of source; reliance on facts and figures that, interpreted by the right ventriloquist, speak for themselves.

In advertising and political campaigning alike, these methods are not only obvious and predictable to the connoisseur — they are coming more and more to be expected by the viewers. A popular TV advertising strategy during the 1960s concentrated on boosting the product via favourable reactions from the man in the street by the 'vox pop' technique. A classic commercial use of 'vox pop' was in an advert for peppermints ('It's a nice little mint . . . it's got a hole that your tongue goes in . . . you get a real minty taste', etc.). But in the event the invariable public support for the product, thus archly expressed, began to ring untrue. It became clear to the least trained of media observers that the 'vox pop' image of a product involved tinkering – that persons regarding the mint as an unpleasant little concoction were screened out of the way. So over-use of the technique bred a resistance to it; and advertisers were forced to devise more subtle approaches – hence the witty 'soft sell' tactics of the 1970s. In political campaigning an identical development has taken place, also spurred by the permanent need to disarm the viewer, to resist his resistance. During the 1970s alone, the hard sell dictatorial delivery by politicians of a straight to camera address has become dated and boring. In the general election campaign of autumn 1974, all manner of party political broadcasting styles were in evidence. The Conservative Party tended to stick conservatively to the tried and tested 'head and shoulders' approach just described; while the other two contenders used all the tricks of the medium they could muster, showing their candidates in appropriately connotative settings (lavish offices, on speeding trains, in policy meetings, followed by admiring hordes), using fast cutting techniques and creating a general impression of vitality. The Liberal Party actually presented a series of 'News from the Liberals' bulletins, using all the stylistics of studio news reporting presumably in the attempt to suggest urgent, but impartial, credibility. (Indeed, it is often only by seeing the stylistics of a medium parodied – as in *Monty Python's Flying Circus*, a poem or piece of music after the style of another artiste or in a good cartoon caricature – that one realises the wealth of meaning in the images one has accepted unquestioningly for so long.)

But once the meaning of a particular stylistic has been rendered transparent, it is no longer of the same persuasive value. And, in commercial contexts at least, a technique even more subtle than the 'soft sell' is becoming apparent as we write: in a 1976 advert for a fortified wine, an autocratic 'rival' wine producer declares fiercely, 'I forbid you to try it'. The gentle humour of soft sell here becomes a more dissonant humour of the hard edge: the intention is less to win an audience identification with the product via the presenter than to bewilder by a double-bind. Humour is still the overt intention, but the persuasive process itself is abundantly more complex. And it remains to be seen whether similar techniques surface in future *political* campaigning on television. The power of the visual cues to credibility on television that our own work has indicated is still not general known: and the persuasive value of static cues to expertise and authority (such as bookshelves, desk, standard lamp, expensive decorations) is thus not yet exhausted. When it is, however, other cues will surely take their place.

For example, an American practice used very occasionally in Britain also consists of having a leading member of the party 'interviewed' by an apparently searching and seemingly hostile interviewer who is ultimately 'won over' (cf. chapter 3). As we have argued earlier, a favourable impression of the interviewee may also be promoted by the edited structuring of an interview, irrespective of what is said; the presentation of the interviewee in profile may lead (for the present at least) to enhanced views of trustworthiness and competence; and, furthermore, the responses of the interviewer (which, of course, become increasingly less 'hostile' as the interview proceeds) may act as cues for the viewer, not only in the same way as the 'audience' reactions that we have examined earlier, but also in a subtler way. For our work showed that simple positivity or simple negativity of audience responses influenced the viewer; and the work of Aronson and Linder (1965) indicates the even more subtle effects of different *sequences* of positivity and negativity which merit further study in this context. Using only auditory information they showed that when an individual began an interaction giving negative assessments about a person and subsequently became more positive, he was seen as liking the person *more* than someone who started positive and remained so. Clore, Wiggins and Itkin (1975) have confirmed the finding using videotape techniques. When taken in conjunction with our work on interviews, it is clear that a changing pattern of interviewer (or audience) reactions may have a considerable influence on the viewers' perceptions of an interviewee. In the context of 'political' interviews (especially in party political broadcasts where such reactions can be rehearsed) the enhancement of candidates, ministers, politicians — and the views that they advocate — may clearly be manipulated without the viewers ever being aware of the fact, because of the depth at which the influence operates.

It is important to see that our explanation of the persuasive influence depends on our earlier analysis of the need for structure, and that, as argued in the discussion of our experiments, it will be most virulent in an environment where complex issues are discussed familiarly, but without the full understanding on the part of the viewer. It is not simply an extension of the process exemplified on the coins of the later Roman emperors, who stamped their image against a background of conquering legions, municipal good works and other politically advantageous associations — for this is merely where the technique *starts*, as it did in advertising. The simple association of product, person, or idea with something positive tends in advertising to supplant normal logic, so that clever association, and the manipulation of associations or symbolic forms, ultimately becomes more fundamental to the process of marketing and persuasion than does the actual product or idea or person that is being presented. In this context the symbolic process then takes on its very own ethical codes. Thus, although one knows what is meant by words like 'honest', 'decent', 'legal' and 'truthful' (the standards which the IBA looks for in all TV advertisements before they are accepted for broadcasting), one can be equally sure that they all carry the rider 'within the context of standard advertising practice'. In consequence, they refer to images of the product, or generalised, untestable claims, rather than to hard fact about it (e.g. 'Doctors recommend . . .', 'Good, clean and natural', 'Probably the world's leading . . .', 'Adds life to your engine . . .', rather than 'contains 0·05 per cent phenylalanine', 'Derived from the intestines of the sperm whale', 'An artificial product composed of the following chemicals . . .', 'Explodes at a different temperature because of a lead additive . . .').

In the context of political broadcasting, acceptance of a similar ethical duality has led, and continues to lead, to an increasing emphasis on symbolic forms of democratic discussion such as 'access TV' (see below), and to a concentration on the images of politicians rather than their actions. Evidently images are far easier to manipulate than actions — which is unfortunate for the uninformed audience — and an increasing acceptance of image variation as a central theme in political debate amounts to an increasing acceptance of the licence to manipulate.

Of course, it is important that the significance of this argument be seen in context: for party political broadcasts on the media are only one of a number of traditional campaigning forms. Yet it is important to note the general point that the influence of TV and TV production methods upon politics is capable of immense development, just as in the field of commercial persuasion it so greatly resembles. If the role of TV in persuasion is considerable today it may become even more so in future; the styles of persuasion will undergo dynamic changes as viewers become sophisticated in the medium's stylistics in general. But the dynamics of television as an art form in its own right are such that a total transparency can always be resisted by those who are skilled in its use. And in news programmes, politics and advertising contexts alike the powers of television for providing the audience with cues for a new structuring of information will continue to unfold. The same function — of providing information within a suggested structure — will be served at the two extremes of the informative function: by the use of TV in propaganda and in education (see chapter 6). Of course it is true that news programmes are not propaganda; nor are they all political; neither are they overt advertisements. But the techniques used by producers are often essentially so similar in all four types of presentation and we have attempted to show that the simple view that news reports 'the facts' whilst other programmes do not is not only naïve but dangerously so. Our analysis is intended to identify a dimension in the analysis of TV presentations which has so far not received the attention from broadcasting authorities that it deserves — not surprisingly in view of the fact that it has been thoroughly neglected in research.

Identification of the power of the techniques and the possibility of their use for deliberate manipulative ends naturally raises ethical considerations. Specifically: are closer controls and closer scrutiny of their use in news and documentary programmes required and is their use ever totally controllable anyway? Additionally, may not their identification present politicians and advertisers with techniques which, whilst used unwittingly until now, can henceforth be exploited? These three issues are clearly interrelated and we shall return to them in the last chapter of the book. One key point is that identification of these effects presents the broadcasting authorities with the opportunity to prevent them. As we have argued before, information helps to structure the environment and the same applies to 'meta-information' about how the production techniques provide structure.

Related to this point is the fact that education *about* the medium is as fundamental as education *through* it, and the proponents of democratic forms may be well-advised to direct some of their attention in future to educating the viewers about the influence of TV itself on their thought processes. Certainly the possibility has been overlooked so far, and whilst we do not suppose that TV broadcasters will wish to transmit information programmes about their own techniques (in the way that the IBA occasionally broadcasts explanations of how it selects advertisements, and then invites viewers' comments or complaints), we do feel that the public would be well served if attention were paid to similar possibilities.

At what level should such education be directed? First, we feel that viewers need to be made aware that such techniques exist and have effects. Secondly, it may be instructive to draw parallels between their unintended and innocuous uses in certain types of broadcasting (cf. the discussion of educational TV in the next chapter) and their intentional and more sinister uses in persuasive television: in other words, something can be gained by placing the techniques in a context. Thirdly, a long term need relates less to the specific views put forward by such techniques and rather more to the general views propounded by the medium *through* such techniques: just as people are now more concerned than they once were over the content of children's stories and with the roles attributed in them to males, females and golliwogs, so too it may be appropriate to consider the implications of TV's view of the world, particularly its approach to documentary, contentious and politically-oriented programmes. Fourthly, the place of TV in education needs to be considered since the techniques outlined earlier could be used to good effect in that context (see chapter 6). The point here is not simply that TV can be used in education: that is obvious. It is the implications of its use which are important. For, as we have argued, TV's informative use is broader than its simple news or documentary function, and it can undoubtedly have an 'educational' impact without meaning to (e.g. by presenting police stories that give details of how crimes have been committed; by presenting violent stories to children; by challenging or supporting certain social mores). It is paradoxical that an emphasis on TV's educational function in itself points to the importance of, and public reliance upon, the medium as an information source: and that it is this very aspect of the medium about which education is required.

Summary

(1)   A general determinist view of the impact of TV sees the viewer as governed by a range of human and social needs summed up as the need for information and a structure by which to interpret it. The diminished social context in which TV is viewed increases the likelihood of viewers' reliance upon the structure it imposes.

(2)   TV itself creates new psychological needs by the way in which it 'sells' its information, a particular image of reality, and thereby sells itself. The persuasive instincts of the TV journalist are essentially the same as those applied in general commercial contexts.

(3)   The depth and dynamic symbolist approaches used by advertisers create an image of credibility for the product via that of its presenters. This process is replicated in the manner by which TV markets opinions presenting both simple and complex information at a level which most may understand.

(4)   The deliberate use of TV presentation strategies for political and propagandist purposes can only be countered by a dynamic resistance on the part of the viewing audience. The audience needs to be kept informed and educated about TV through constant scrutiny of its techniques and

their potential effects.

References

Argyle, M. (1964), *Psychology and Social Problems*, London, Methuen.

Aronson, E. (1973), *The Social Animal*, London, Freeman.

Aronson, E. and Linder, D. (1965), 'Gain and loss of esteem as determinants of interpersonal attractiveness', *J. Exper. Soc. Psychol.*, vol. 1.

Clore, J., Wiggins, N. H. and Itkin, S. (1975), 'Gain and loss in attraction: attribution from non-verbal behaviour', *J. Pers. Soc. Psychol.*, vol. 31.

Festinger, L. (1954), 'A theory of social comparison processes', *Human Relations*, vol. 7.

Geertsma, R. H. and Reivich, R. S. (1969), 'Auditory and visual dimensions of externally mediated self-observation', *J. Nerv. Ment. Dis.*, vol. 148.

Glasser, R. (1967), *The New High Priesthood*, London, Macmillan.

Himmelweit, H., Oppenheim, A. and Vince, P. (1958), *Television and the Child*, New York, Oxford University Press.

Kelvin, P. (1970), *The Bases of Social Behaviour*, London, Holt Rinehart.

Lasswell, H. D. (1927), 'A theory of political propaganda', *Amer. Pol. Sci. Review*, vol. 21.

Lifton, R. J. (1961), *Thought Reform and the Psychology of Totalism: A Study of "Brainwashing" in China*, New York, Norton.

Packard, V. (1964), *The Hidden Persuaders*, Harmondsworth, Penguin.

Peterson, R., Jensen, J. W. and Rivers, W. L. (1965), *The Mass Media in Society*, New York, Holt Rinehart.

Qualter, T. H. (1968), *Propaganda and Psychological Warfare*, New York, Random House.

Secord, P. and Backman, C. W. (1974), *Social Psychology*, New York, McGraw-Hill.

Wheldon, Sir H. (1976), The Richard Dimbleby Lecture (BBC-2); and *The Listener*, 4 March.

Wreford, R. J. R. G. (1923), 'Propaganda, evil and good', *The Nineteenth Century and After*, 93.

6   Television and education

In the previous chapter we argued the lack of any basis on which to distinguish effectively between persuasive and informative processes; the profound influence within both of the presenter's credibility upon the way in which the message is received; and the connection on this basis between education and actual forms of propaganda. In recent years both educational and propagandist uses of television have become increasingly possible with the development of closed circuit TV technology and greater freedom of access by private individuals and groups to the public television networks. In the present chapter we discuss the growth of 'access television' and educational technology specifically, and point to the need for closer study of television's properties and effects if its potential in either context is to be realised. The organisation of a theoretical discipline capable of allowing the study of communication and media processes in their own right is next indicated. The subject area is multi-disciplinary, and demands the development of new research techniques for an examination of communication processes from the psychodynamic as well as determinist viewpoints. The practical value of simulation techniques in this respect is discussed; and in the final sections of the chapter the potential role of semiology in communication studies is indicated. Stemming from linguistics, this approach requires certain modifications if it is to be applied in the study of psychological processes, and we indicate the value of probability theory in this connection.

Access television

Our definition of persuasion on television has implied a style of use whereby the medium serves interests other than those of the viewer. Definitions of education, on the other hand, imply the use of communication channels in the recipient's interest specifically. The educational use of television may therefore be defined as that which intends to serve the viewer's interests by providing him with specific benefits. Of course, the definition of educational benefit will ultimately be subjective; and a working distinction between persuasion and education need not concern us in this or any other context, since it is bound to be elusive. At the nexus between forms of persuasion and education as commonly understood, however, we may observe numerous communication forms. A leading example of television's use to communicate material of this intermediate type during the 1970s has been apparent in the 'access' to the medium by amateur users. Political and popular pressures on the broadcasting organisations to provide public airtime on demand have been described by Groombridge (1972), while the case for democratic participation in the media was espoused by Anthony Wedgwood Benn, then Minister of Technology in 1968: 'Broadcasting', he said, 'is really too important to be left to the broadcasters.' This maxim has been held as the origin for the flood of popular access activities that has followed. Most of the British television companies have in one way or another made available their facilities to individuals or to minority social groups appealing for it. The request for airtime is now not only seen as acceptable, but also as a necessary way in which the media can display a social conscience and responsibility. Whether the broadcasters like it or not, the effort is on to 'demystify the medium' as surely as the Emperor was denuded of his new clothes.

But in view of the extent to which the properties of television as a communication tool are an unknown quantity even to those whose skill in its use is maximal, is access to the medium by amateur users likely to have any unpredicted effects? At a time when the potency of television effects is only gradually becoming apparent, is general access to media techniques a premature and rather dangerous development? The beneficial effects of experimentation with television in therapeutic work are considerable (Brenes, 1975). Through objectifying personal and group problems in a media context, strategies may be organised and a solution arrived at. The process is nonetheless a hesitant one, for however persuasive the use of television, it still readily arouses suspicion. A two-year old child, on seeing its father depicted there, will retreat from its initial recognition to cling to the real image for assurance. An active relationship between viewers and the medium must be established if actual reorganisation is to result.

In the Canadian pioneering work with access television, its particular strength in community contexts has been observed. Through gradual access to production skills and a persistence in bringing them to the notice of authorities, radical local reforms are obtained. The effects are achieved *in camera*, closed circuit: access to the airwaves is unnecessary if the intended audience can be identified and isolated. The broadcast use of access is justified if the audience is diffuse: and recent examples of the vogue in Britain have achieved notable results in transmitting advice on general themes of political and medical self-help. The purpose of much other access broadcasting has been less clearly defined: Edward Goldwyn (1974), producer of the BBC-TV *Open Door* series, acknowledges that few single programmes probably have any real effect. Indeed, in aiming the production at an audience far broader than required, it is possible that many groups achieve far less of an effect through access than they might have done. Are there other dangers? In the hands of the semi-skilled media worker, can television serve to damage his cause, frustrating the attempt at self-expression rather than creating new opportunities as expected?

From the immense complexity of the production and viewing processes indicated earlier it is clear that the possibilities for undesired effects when television is used by amateurs are infinite. Variations in production, editing and performance technique are each shown to exert potentially far-reaching effects on the way the television message is interpreted. The extent to which total freedom should be granted to the amateur user to produce, edit and present his own material should therefore certainly be questioned. In certain circumstances it is likely that total access may be desirable in every respect, while in others this would be ill-advised. The point is exemplified by reference to three access programmes broadcast by Granada-TV in January 1975. The first, *Take Us To Our Leaders,* described an exercise conducted during the general election campaign of October 1974 in which a statistical cross-section of voters took part in a series of programmes culminating in a question and answer session with each of the three main party leaders. Since the professional mediators maintained control over the production and editing processes throughout this exercise, actual access to the medium was strictly limited to the interviewing role alone; interestingly, the only reservation of the participants regarding the success of the venture concerned the fact that professional interviewers could have fulfilled this role better. When the informative aim of a TV programme is general in scope, there is clearly little to be gained by involving unskilled media users in this way. Where freedom of access can often be justified, however, is in the attempt to inform the public on individual or group issues which are more specific in nature.

A second film by Granada-TV, *Cleveland House*, was a case in point. The subjects of the film were the day residents at a mental home, who had requested the opportunity to correct a previous image which they felt the medium had given them. The decision to grant the patients access to the medium in every respect — including use of the cameras and sound equipment, and design of the eventual edited sequences — proved well-founded. The programme resulting from this policy was a simple transcription of the daily routine at the home, and an effective counter to

136

the popular stereotype of the mentally ill. All concerned were satisfied with it (though it should be noted that professional control over the product was still partially necessary, for without additional commentary explaining the programme's development much of the amateur-produced material would merely have bewildered with possible distressing effects to the users). The extent to which provision of total access may lead to a completely unsatisfactory product is exemplified in the third film, *Kirkby: A Self Portrait.* Again the aim of the programme was for a particular community — residents in a suburban new town — to present its own public image, thus redressing that painted by the media generally; and again the amateur participants were given full control over the filming, presentation and subsequent editing processes. The result was a confused and factious account of Kirkby's image, which in subsequent discussion (Baggaley, 1975; Collins, 1975) proved as unsatisfactory to the Kirkby residents as the image generally projected. In granting access to an extreme degree, without careful anticipation of its possible risks, the media unwittingly exacerbated the problems of the community and intensified the arguments between its sub-groups. In the light of the psychological effects of television discussed earlier, the failure of this latter venture might actually have been avoided. Since television's powers of imagery derive mainly from implication and inference rather than from logical argument, skills of verbal persuasion are inadequate when used on their own. If an image is to be changed through argument rather than by example, the techniques of media control must first be learned. The risks of any total access to the medium are clear from the evidence that even experienced media controllers may not realise all the psychological effects their techniques exert. Since much of televised content seems to receive our less than total attention, often failing to register in a conscious fashion at all, the chance of achieving a positive effect on the basis of isolated transmissions is in any case slender — and in the preparations for any access venture this should be the first warning.

Indeed, as a safeguard in the provision of media access generally, the present firm stipulations that the facility shall not be used to advertise, defame or incite should be extended. The aim of an access project must be clearly defined, and the advantages of broadcast vs closed circuit transmission carefully weighed. If broadcasting organisations really want to display a social responsibility they might encourage use of their facilities on a closed circuit basis where appropriate. In broadcast work, the right of final decision should be retained by professional staff on every matter bearing on the programme's aim — and these should be defined (presentation, sequence, detail, etc.). In particular, media control over the editing and presentation processes should be guarded. Otherwise, the use of access involves certain risks. The user is frustrated in his aims and disappointed with his self-image: when a self-portrait is attempted on canvas with no previous access to paints or brushes, the result is rarely as satisfying as a professional portrait, and usually less so. But when due control over the medium is retained by those accustomed to it, collaboration with amateur users may still be fruitful. *Akenfield* was 'made by the people of Suffolk' and regarded as their own property, even though it was 'Peter Hall's film' also. The heightened awareness of self and group identities that results from much access can certainly be beneficial. But when the controls are relinquished, the distortions that television produces may lead to an introspective crisis which the users have no opportunity to resolve.

The problem of control over television's dynamics is the prime question which must be tackled before its future development as a socially valuable tool may be ensured. From a basis of ignorance as to its properties, as we have seen, the use of television for social benefit may be offset by a number of negative effects. The problem is even more apparent when television is used for overt educational effects than it is in its campaigning usage. In the next section we examine the uses to which television has been put in education proper during the revolution in educational technology that has taken place since the early 1960s.

Television as teacher

The organised use of television as an educational tool is epitomised in Great Britain by the development that Sir Harold Wilson has regarded as his greatest achievement: the Open University, however, is only one of numerous educational organisations in Britain and overseas which in recent years have come to use the medium of television as an alternative to the older media of blackboard and chalk. Universities, polytechnics, colleges, and schools alike are now equipped with a sophisticated range of media facilities. The desire of teachers to develop the media skills hitherto practised by a privileged few is a version of the desire to demystify the medium that we have already examined. The closed circuit use of television in education is thus in itself a form of the 'access' phenomenon: as such it promises distinct benefits for the educational user, though in its development during the 1960s and 1970s it has suffered the same problems that we now predict for the access television developments of the future, namely those stemming from an inability to predict and control the medium's psychological benefits.

The development of closed circuit television (CCTV) facilities in higher education may be traced back to the Brynmor Jones report (1965) which advocated the use of audio-visual aids in science teaching specifically. At present, the responsibility for applying the innovating technologies in education, and for realising their full potential, rests with a relatively small band of devotees. In higher educational institutions, their aims have typically been recognised by the foundation of central service units, each with a particular commitment to the use of film, television and tape/slide systems. During its initial stages of development, the service unit's main task is to explain its facilities to the rest of the institution, and to compare the cost of its services with their value. An early model for the development of audio-visual aids units in the British universities was established at the University of Liverpool in 1967 (Leytham, 1970). General uses of the educational media are exemplified in the following analysis of Liverpool's CCTV activities during an — albeit atypical — five-month period (Baggaley, 1972).

In all, twenty-seven individual lecturers belonging primarily to the departments of Medicine, Education, and Extension Studies commissioned twenty-nine distinct jobs — long term projects as well as the more commonplace one-off items. 59 per cent of the videotapes produced contained usually inaccessible material, 34 per cent provided magnification of material, and 52 per cent enabled subsequent re-analysis of, for example, situations in which the apparatus permitted unobtrusive observation (28 per cent). As a medium for assembling aural and visual information from various sources, CCTV is little in demand (34 per cent of material), and only eight members of the total University staff (30 per cent of those who used the services during this period) actually requested any kind of formal production. Occasional demands (28 per cent each) were made for the instantaneous relay of information and for playback facilities solving, for instance, a lecture theatre's overflow problem. Only four jobs (14 per cent of the total) involved 'off-air recording', though subsequent work at Liverpool suggests that this proportion was atypical. And as the nature of the services becomes better known the demand for all of them has greatly increased.

Yet clearly not all teachers embrace the new aids with equal enthusiasm and it is too easy to blame this on misguided conservatism. For the benefits currently derived from educational technology are still remarkably limited. While the technical resources multiply, the methods for using them remain capricious and arbitrary; while concentrating on the design of gadgetry, technologists have failed to establish their educational value.

139

It is still a technology without techniques, and as such its future influence remains uncertain.

In her review of its usage in higher education, Zeckhauser (1972) outlines technology's original promise and the reasons for its present failure to develop as a coherent discipline. Confusion in the marketing of educational machinery combines with an inability to master the main problems that educationalists face. Indeed, the needs that educational technologists have aimed to meet in their campaign for technical innovation have been far too restricted. There are more fundamental problems to be solved within education than overcrowding in the lecture theatre, and wide sections of university and college staff require neither to magnify materials nor to re-analyse them. More concerned with the problems of effectively communicating less tangible information than a slide or graph can show, they have no need for the present forms of audio-visual aid at all. And if the vision of future developments is to be more than a pipe-dream, educational technologists must now examine the more general problems and decide whether they can offer solutions.

If, as seems apparent, future strain within the educational system will be greater than human resources alone can overcome, we should first consider the functions of a teacher, and ways in which the media can relieve some of the pressures by simulating these functions. Baggaley (1973b) has defined four major teaching functions as follows:

(1)   The ability to present a logically developing sequence of information;
(2)   Awareness of the need to reinforce information either by repetition or by presenting the material in alternative forms;
(3)   The capacity to establish a relationship with the class; and
(4)   A capacity to cope with the problems of individual students.

In order that the educational media may accomplish such functions, principles of instruction must be applied in the design of methodology: the analysis of objectives is of little value until the presentation procedures by which they are achieved can be defined.

The type of presentation variables traditionally thought to influence media effectiveness (speed of delivery, mode and length of presentation, etc.) is discussed by Moss (1972). Producers in educational television appear to have either disregarded the principles offered by previous research workers, or to have developed their own intuitive criteria for production effectiveness which may or may not be appropriate in the educational context. The findings bearing on length of presentation must frequently have been ignored; for, as Moss states,

... published catalogues of videotapes already recorded show many examples which run over 25 minutes, although psychologists have long known that the average span of attention, even for highly motivated students, is unlikely to exceed 20–25 minutes. (p.2)

Of course, it is possible that it is the researchers who are wrong in offering such principles, culled in the rarified atmosphere of the psychological laboratory, as necessarily relevant in the media context at all. For a TV producer may certainly vary the rate and the mood of his programme so as to promote more efficient learning over a longer period. The possible variations of production technique in this way are actually infinite. Baggaley (1973a) indicates that numerous production options conventionally applied for the sole purpose of sustaining the visual interest of a programme may also be used for educational effects previously unforeseen. To this end new rules for their use must be established on the basis of organised research into their precise psychological effects; and the unwitting side-effects of presentation that only research can reveal are as potentially valuable in this context as the more predictable ones.

The investigations of presentation effect reported in chapter 4 are each examples of the type of research that may immediately be harnessed in the educational interest. On present evidence at least, it would, for example, appear that the first of the four major teaching functions – the ability to present a logically developing sequence of information – may be fulfilled by more careful attention to the edited structure of a presentation, and to the side-effects seen to be associated with particular editing techniques. In fact our findings go so far as to suggest that certain types of information may be more effectively taught by the use of interview techniques than by the 'talking head' presentation styles conventionally used. (Research as to the subject matter most susceptible to this kind of treatment is now required.) Since qualities of expertise and reliability are evidently suggested more effectively in interview situations than by a direct address to camera, one may consider that the most favourable reactions of a class to television performers may be elicited by avoiding the use of straight to camera addresses altogether. (One British University TV service (Creaser, 1976) intuitively avoids the visual presentation of the lecturer wherever possible, considering it distracting from and generally quite irrelevant to the subject matter being taught: our research suggests that this quite unusual intuition on the part of an ETV producer is indeed well founded.) Further psychological research may prove that many of the more common intuitions in ETV production are less substantiated than is generally assumed: but it must of course take carefully into account our earlier observations that the language of television and its effects are constantly evolving, the response of the viewing audience to it developing at the same dynamic rate. As we saw in chapter 2, it is generally necessary in the entertainment use of a medium to keep one step ahead of the viewer, constantly devising new techniques to replace the old ones to which he has become accustomed. Viewing interest is thus kept preoccupied by the constant variety and unpredictability of the medium in a way that often suggests the viewing involvement to be actually quite passive. However, in educational contexts the attention and involvement of the audience must at all times be active or only the most superficial aspects of the message will be recalled; and the need to check thoroughly the suitability of conventional TV presentation techniques for educational use, and to devise new ways of using the medium educationally as the usual criteria are seen to be wanting, is indicated on this basis alone. The surest way to encourage active involvement in the television message will be to develop methods by which the intentions underlying the television message are effectively signposted in the way they are presented. The simple logic of the cut or fade, for instance, which in general filmic contexts may be used to suggest quite complicated notions of spatial relationship or the passage of time, can be applied more consciously in the emphasis of a programme's equally complex conceptual structure. In 'zooming in', similarly, the ETV producer has not only a tool for the magnification of objects, but also a device for directing attention to a significant point; while in 'zooming out' he can imply that, for example, notes may now be taken while the speaker makes a few redundant comments designed to draw a section of his exposition to a close. In situations where an interview presentation is clearly inappropriate, therefore, presentation skills may thus be used to overcome the otherwise impersonal nature of the medium by imitating signals passed during human interaction (as indicated in chapter 3), in the consequent development of a simulated interpersonal relationship between the studio presenter and his audience, and in interpreting programme content on the audience's behalf.

In ETV production generally an applied knowledge of the interpretation process discussed in chapter 3 is thus of prime importance; and effective ETV presentation strategy is one which takes this into account in coding the message in its mediated form. It is essential also to remember that information must also be capable of decoding before it can be assimilated — a fact that producers quite often overlook. In a series of experiments by Webster and Cox (1973), for example, the use of colour coding to denote the instructional importance of TV captions was examined. Most students failed to use the distinctions in colour in perceiving the captions at all, and unless the code was specifically explained to them before presentation it proved quite ineffective. Unless TV producers deliberately educate the viewer in the decoding of their message, therefore, the efficiency of communication between them will be impaired; but when appropriately informed of presentation strategies by a process akin to the tuition of visual literacy, audiences will ultimately become as adept at understanding the codes pertaining to higher conceptual relationships and the communication of ideas as they are to those expressing relationships of space and time in more conventional usage.

A useful assumption to apply in general ETV research and development is thus that a student has little initial motivation to learn from the material we presented to him, but that this stems from his ability to handle the material as it unfolds. Skills of TV decoding serve not only to permit the viewer to appreciate the ways the medium is used by its producers, but also to motivate him to use it to maximum advantage himself. Viewing 'skills' may clearly be defined in precisely the same way as the skills of teaching, and in educational technology generally the prospect of their practical definition opens immense new possibilities. For in coming not only to understand the manner in which individual responses to learning materials differ, but also ways in which members of an audience may be instructed to act similarly, a philosophical base is gained for the development of more effective group instruction methods as well as the self-instruction and personal access methodology to which the discipline has become primarily committed; and in an educational system already groaning under increasing student numbers and dwindling funds, attention to the improvement of group teaching procedures using existing resources is certainly to be commended, from logistic as well as commonsense points of view. When a group of small children is taught to play the violin, they exhibit numerous initial differences in bowing style and fingering accuracy: but differently shaped violins are not then constructed to cater for these differences. Instead, ways are found to overcome the pupils' initial problems by giving them skills in the use of the instrument — any other approach would be defeatist and ultimately defeated. Likewise, by educating their audience as to the specific presentation codes in use, the ETV producer will become able to develop the dynamic capabilities of the medium and its viewers simultaneously, *ipso facto* adopting a far more realistic approach to educational problems than ever apparent in educational technology hitherto.

Television studies

The growth in our understanding of television's dynamic properties and the pragmatic approach to its effective usage in social contexts are ultimately to be organised by the formulation of an organised discipline for the study of communication processes in their own right. The significance of such a discipline would be equally recognised in both academic and applied contexts, in areas of occupational and vocational guidance in the press, the media and commercial fields generally. All communication, as we have argued in earlier chapters, is in one respect or another mediated. In studying the communication process we are thus specifically concerned with the effects of message mediation, whether or not the medium is of a technological form such as television: equally capable of study as media are people, language, music, carrier pigeons, and the air we breathe. In education the need for new media methods improving and guaranteeing the effectiveness of teacher/student communication was commendably indicated by the programmed learning specialists (cf. Kay, Dodd and Sime, 1968). They recognised that communication, being essentially a two-way process, is incomplete if the student is not actively involved in the process of learning, if he does not receive continual knowledge of his progress and remedial treatment in the event of error (Baggaley, Jamieson and Marchant, 1975). The communication principles from psychology, engineering, and cybernetics on which many modern educational methods are based form the partial substance of a science of communication that we now see in development.

Since the early and mid-1970s, courses in Communication have been offered by several British polytechnics and colleges, with particular orientation towards an engineering/cybernetic model or to the applied issues of journalism or graphic art. The wide number of subject areas to which the blanket term 'Communication' has been applied indicates not only the diversity of existing attempts to get such a discipline organised, but also the wealth of interdisciplinary inputs by which the new discipline may be justified. In their integration, however, the question arises as to whether communication is essentially a science, an art, or a technology. The question was effectively posed by Cherry (1973) in a seminal address on the discipline's potential. It is unavoidable that the interpretations of a discipline concerning communication may be as varied as the applications which it serves: in the United States and Australia, for example, a wide range of variants on the theme according to different art, science, and journalistic orientations is already apparent (cf. Mohan, 1976). In Britain the development has been far slower: only two British universities currently provide undergraduate courses in the discipline, and these already reflect the opposite extremes of its applied gamut (at Heriot-Watt University, it is based explicitly on the engineering flow model; at the University of Liverpool it emphasises arts and social scientific applications).

Within both frameworks, new possibilities are opened for the study of communication media, the techniques used in media production, their effects and the development of skills for the more effective control of the media in future contexts. Educational and propagandist mediation become the proper subject matter of communication studies on an equivalent basis; and it is on this organised base that we may look for the guidance needed by those who would more effectively control media processes for social effect. Unfortunately, in education the problems which media such as television have attempted to redress are immediate, and the evolution of general principles of communication effectiveness becomes a matter of urgency (Baggaley and Duck, 1975a). In order to sensitise teachers, researchers and students to the effects and techniques of television presentation, procedures of the type devised by Masterman (1976) are to be recommended.

In a course of television studies designed for fifteen-year-old comprehensive school pupils, Masterman has developed a simulation exercise highlighting aspects of television journalism. Having first acquired basic production skills, the students are allowed a short period in which to prepare a TV news and current affairs bulletin. The pressures of daily television journalism and the live transmission deadline are carefully built into the simulation schedule and from this exercise the coping skills and the inevitable biases introduced by the constraints of the television situation become readily apparent. The types of debate that may be enlivened by such an approach are summarised by Masterman as follows:

(1)   Does the news present us with an accurate picture of what the real world is like?
(2)   Why do unpleasant, odd or exciting occurrences play such an important part in the news?
(3)   How does television make its news events more dramatic and exciting?
(4)   How are news events which might be quite long and complicated to explain presented on television?
(5)   How far is preference given to stories simply because they have a strong visual appeal?
(6)   How is each item in the news broadcast presented so as to make the

maximum impact?

The benefits of such an approach are clearly not restricted to the teaching of older student age-groups.

The recent (1976) Granada-TV series *The Messengers* has been teaching the effects of bias through editing and other production manoeuvres in a manner suitable for children aged about twelve. It is feasible that such material may soon become staple fare within the junior school curriculum also, for the 1970s generation of children is exposed to and versed in the visual codes of television and film to a degree unknown when their parents were children. As one of the present authors' children has shown, a child may recognise a familiar television jingle before it can even speak, and the musical literacy which this implies is a mark of far greater sensitivity to the properties of the media than his parents will probably ever attain without intense concentration. The creative and interpretative skills of the visual media are potentially as vital a subject for study at all levels of education as those of the literary media were before them. And the purview of media studies includes not only those factors underlying the psycho-dynamic effects of the media, but also those organisational, social and cultural factors that have fallen outside our current province in this volume.

It is clear that the technological developments of recent years have provided us with closed circuit facilities capable of use not only for applied training purposes, but also in the interests of the purer forms of research. Experiments such as we have described in chapter 4 would have been possible at no earlier time, for the prime requisite of experimental design — that all variables except the ones under study are effectively held constant — would have been impossible to guarantee in the present context before the electronic technology was available. As recently as 1975, it was indicated by Hooper that the problem of holding constant all but one of the many variables affecting interpersonal communication at any one time is all but impossible. For communication is full of unknown idiosyncracies. Even now, however, we know that given appropriate TV recording facilities this conclusion may be unnecessarily pessimistic; and the application of television techniques in the experimental study of human interaction processes underlying, for example, leadership training, personnel management and counselling henceforward will add a new freedom to the types of question that may be tackled.

A note of warning to the student of television processes must, however, be added at this point. As we have indicated in the section concerning educational technology, effects established in the psychological laboratory

146

have been assumed without question or testing to apply within media research also. Thus the findings of vigilance investigations that human performance in a monotonous and repetitive task deteriorates after about twenty minutes (Mackworth, 1970) has been popularly applied by educational researchers to show that twenty minutes is the maximum length for an effective educational broadcast (cf. Moss, 1972). The failure to allow that manipulation of a programme's presentation characteristics will naturally overcome this basic effect further testifies to the lack of attention previously paid to presentation factors. The abstraction of psychological variables from their traditional context is thus to be undertaken with extreme caution: indeed, the traditional laboratory settings in which variables are isolated are themselves often suspect. For, as we have indicated in chapter 4, experimental variables manipulated in isolation may appear to exercise a highly significant effect, though their role in reality is only seen in interaction with other variables. It is important, therefore, that the effects of any TV presentation technique examined singly be checked against its effects in the more realistic media situations wherein individual techniques are combined (cf. the 'appeal' experiment). In research conducted in the name of media studies henceforward, it will be important to ensure that the interacting variables of, for example, mediated performance, interaction style, visual and aural presentation are carefully held constant in turn, but also observed in juxtaposition.

In connection with the specific presentation effects we have reported numerous variables for further research are indicated. Indeed, the effects established to date are clearly an infinitely small selection of those operating *in toto*. We may consider, for example, the effects on an audience of, amongst other things:

(1) Styles of camera—eye contact used by performers;
(2) Studio settings and their effects on the interaction between performers;
(3) Styles of camera direction in the representation of a performance or interaction;
(4) The degree of correspondence between audio and visual images; and
(5) The effects of music on the interpretation of material.

Each of these avenues in turn relates to broader issues of, for example, interview and performance strategy governed by the actual participants in the televised material. From chapter 3 and the previous section we have seen that studies of this nature may feed directly upon the plentiful tradition of attitude research within social psychology. But it should be re-emphasised that practical guidance for the more effective government of communication techniques in a modern television situation must be based on actual study of that situation itself. The dynamics of television's impact demand that research into its effective usage be constantly checked and updated. And although certain of the effects we have reported here are essentially similar to others identified previously by such pioneers as Eisenstein, Kuleshov, and Pudovkin (chapter 1), their study will continue to be justified for as long as the dynamic development of televisual form continues.

In the final sections of this chapter we therefore suggest a theoretical framework by which not only the static effects of a communication medium may be described, but which accommodates also the very dynamics of their fluctuation and change.

Semiology

As we observed at the outset, various theoretical models have been applied in the analysis of communication processes, and the study of perceptual factors underlying all psychological processes was one of the basic avenues along which psychology developed from the physical and philosophical sciences during the nineteenth century. Terminology for describing the relationship of factors in the communication process was devised by signal detection and information theorists since the war, and an area that we have not hitherto discussed – the examination of imagery factors operating from within the psychological system – has gained respectability since the early 1960s (Holt, 1964): this latter area though, never integrated within communication theory proper, must certainly become so if it is to be fully manipulable henceforth. A shortcoming of each of these areas, however, as of traditional psychological thinking generally, has been their inability to express the dynamics underlying psychological factors, the lability of one factor in relation to another, and the collision of two separate factors to form a third. The tendency to copy empirical styles from the physical sciences, and to factorise at all, has led on the one hand to a prematurely rigid style of empirical thought, and on the other to a loosely defined vocabulary of little value in prediction. Of course each of these qualities is quite alien to a pragmatic scientific approach, so that, even collectively (as they stand), they offer little help in the attempt to place the dynamics of television on a working research basis.

Within an entirely different field, however, that of language and linguistics itself, a fundamental concern with the fluidity of language and its applications has led to an awareness of its dynamic properties which is unhampered by the calcification that occurs in psychological thought. Linguists too have attempted to understand the relationship of factors underlying communication and the ways in which significance is attributed to a message in the course of its transmission. The recent application of structural linguistic techniques in the analysis of the television message has been examined in chapter 2: while, for example, Proppian analysis (1958) represents the traditional emphasis on the elements of narrative content in a medium (whether literary or visual), the more recent Metzian analysis of cinematic form (1974) emphasises the visual language by which the message is expressed.

Propp and Metz represent the two sides of a linguistic tradition that dates back intermittently to the beginning of the present century. The distinction between separate emphases in message analysis upon (what we have chosen to call) its theme and mediated form was made by Hjelmslev (1963). The latter drew a simple line between the *content* of a message and its *expression*. In propounding the distinction between content and expression, however, linguistic analysts encounter the primary problem of their interdependency. Hjelmslev attempted to resolve this problem by speaking of each in terms of its *substance* and its *form*. This device compels us to refer to the following four message categories:

(1)　The substance of the content (i.e. the narrative elements stemming from the background culture);
(2)　The form of the content (i.e. the semantic structure which is added to the cultural content);
(3)　The substance of the expression (i.e. the physical images, aural and/or visual, through which the message is transmitted); and
(4)　The form of the expression (the manner in which the physical substances are structured syntactically – the category specifically developed by Metz in his 'grande syntagmatique').

By its very reliance on structural principles, unfortunately, Hjelmslev's analysis leads into the theoretical impasse we discussed in chapter 2: the analysis of content and expression in similar terms of structure alone ultimately adds nothing to our knowledge of their relationship. (Nor are we able on this basis to predict the dynamic fashion in which their relationship may change.) For a clearer and more fundamental statement of the problems involved in communication we may return to the origins of the linguistic approach – to the work of Ferdinand de Saussure.

De Saussure's *Course in General Linguistics* (1915) tackled the very problem that linguists and psychologists have tried with less success to treat ever since: the process by which a message conveys meaning. De Saussure saw the need for an exhaustive scientific study of the communication of meaning, one that would define the types of meaningful 'sign' and symbol occurring in nature, and the manner in which they become recognised as such:

> A science that studies the life of signs within society is conceivable; it would be part of social psychology and consequently of general psychology; I shall call it *semiology* (from the Greek 'semeion', sign). Semiology would show what constitutes signs, what laws govern them. Since the science does not yet exist, no one can say what it would be; but it has a right to existence, a place staked out in advance. Linguistics is only a part of the general science of semiology; the laws discovered by semiology will be applicable to linguistics, and the latter will circumscribe a well-defined area within the mass of anthropological facts. (cf. Wollen, 1974, pp.116–17)

The various media of communication, de Saussure thus indicated, are governed by the same semiological laws, capable of analysis in fundamentally similar terms. While the sound or visual display conveying meaning is the *signifier*, the meaning it conveys becomes the *signified*, and the two unite as the *sign* (the signifier and the signified are the two variables developed in more complex terms by Hjelmslev as 'expression' and 'content' and treated variously by later linguistic analysts). The processes whereby meaning is attached to a sign by those who perceive it is in de Saussure's terms primarily governed by its 'arbitrariness', the logical extent to which it reflects the idea signified. On the one hand, a sign may suggest 'the signified' to a highly accurate degree – as a photograph of a face may capture the facial characteristics it mediates – and in Saussurian terminology a sign which signifies the signified to a high degree in this way is a 'motivated' sign. On the other hand, words (linguistic signs suggesting objects and ideas in, for example, an aural form) may have no natural connection with the signified at all, and in de Saussure's terminology are thus arbitrary, or 'unmotivated'.

While de Saussure's terminology expresses the distinction between the signifier and signified quite valuably, it remained for a second linguist, C. S. Pierce, to refine the semiological vocabulary to a level where the varieties of sign and significance might be expressed more fully. A sign, argues Pierce (1955), may be either an icon, an index, or a symbol. An icon represents the object signified by dint of actual physical similarity. The physical image of a TV newsreader is, so we assume, an effective iconic sign of the newsreader himself. An index of a person, on the other

150

hand, is suggestive of him to a lesser degree. In discussing the index, Pierce gives the example of a man 'with a rolling gait': the connotations of his walk may suggest, by the dimension of movement alone, that he is a particular man, or a particular type of man such as a sailor. (Certain gestures, inflections or eye movements of the TV newsreader give indices of his reliability and authority in this way, but the probability that these connotations are reliable is often open to debate.) The connection between an object or idea and the third type of sign, the symbol, contains the least natural logic of all. Corresponding to de Saussure's arbitrary, unmotivated sign, a symbol suggests the object signified for no more logical reason than that of its conventional association with the object. The association of particular visual backgrounds, audience reactions and camera angles with the performers seen in our experiments (chapter 4) enters the symbolic realm accordingly.

The descriptive features of Pierce's trichotomy are its most valuable facet. Its disadvantages are well in evidence: the fact that overlapping between categories may occur (as in any taxonomy, cf. chapter 2), the conflict between the use of a language of probability in the trichotomy ('I see a man with a rolling gait. That is a probable indication that he is a sailor'), and the fact that the probabilities of a sign's particular connotations are subject to dynamic variation over time. Pierce's model fails to take into account the fact that:

(1)   A sign which is quite unmotivated as far as the individual is concerned may have been motivated on his behalf by external influences, e.g. in a training programme (by use of the various sensitisation procedures described earlier in this chapter, for example, we have already indicated that the TV viewer may be alerted to presentation effects to which he was previously oblivious; and
(2)   Over time the meaning of a sign can come to exert influences within the individual's thought at all three levels of Pierce's classification independently.

The perceived meaning of an individual sign may vary substantially depending on psychodynamic factors beyond the individual's control — as Bruner and Goodman (1947) showed in their experiments on the effect of need on, for example, the perceived size of coins (cf. chapter 3) and as E. L. Kelly (1934) demonstrated in his artificial induction of colour tone synaesthesia by a conditioning technique. Apparently quite arbitrary connections between the signifier and the signified may attain an eidetic significance (Jaensch, 1930) as implicit as the relationship between signs and meaning at the iconic level. So, again, *no one sign can by definition be iconic, indexical or symbolic*, for its meaning, as that of the television message at all its levels, naturally varies according to the experience and mental capacity of the individual perceiving it.

The assumption by semiologists such as Pierce, and subsequently by Bazin and Barthes (chapter 1) that a sign at its most iconic truly expresses the reality of the underlying idea in its entirety (as a 'transparent medium') is actually strangely naïve. As we have seen in chapter 1, the tenet that man's perception of the world is at best a personal and shadowy reflection of its true quality has been upheld in philosophy since Plato advanced his theory of forms. Since even de Saussure acknowledged that no sign is likely to be wholly arbitrary, it is curious that he failed to concede that it could never be totally motivated ('iconic'). Indeed, the inadequacies of previous semiological models in relation to human communication theory is highlighted by the emphasis on the selective and organising functions of the brain laid throughout psychological theory. And this major inconsistency in semiological thought has since led to paradoxes such as that pointed out by Wollen (1974). The image presented by an icon, he indicates, is

> . . . 'a kind of natural being-there' of the object. There is no human intervention, no transformation, no code between the object and the sign, hence the paradox that a photograph is a message without a code. (p.124)

Yet even a photograph presents a coded (two-dimensional) version of the (three-dimensional) world; and its decoding requires an understanding of the transformation gathered over time: witness the frequent observations by social anthropologists that primitive tribes fail to recognise the meaning of photographs and filmic images on first encountering them (Carpenter, 1976). We have seen that the language of TV imagery similarly comprises a set of codes. On this basis, of course, the paradox perpetuated by semiologists believing in the true icon's natural occurrence does not arise. And even if we are content to retain Pierce's trichotomy of signs for its great descriptive value, it is evident that we must still add a further dimension to the scheme taking the relationship between external influences on the comprehension of meaning into account. And we should certainly allow within any revision of the scheme for the variation of significance over time.

Media dynamics and probability

A working model for the dynamic processes of media, on which basis the effects of television may not only be described but ultimately predicted, monitored and controlled, thus needs a new language. The rigidity of the language in which communication processes have traditionally been discussed must be replaced by a set of terms more appropriately flexible, and these must permit the measurement of media effects in permanent flux. The messages and meaning mediated by television may be seen descriptively in semiological terms; and we may note particularly the freedom these provide us to analyse the communication process from both the sender's and the receiver's point of view. But in order to describe the different effects of television on individuals and over time, we must be able to reconcile the various influences on the transmission of its message within a single framework.

The conflict between external and internal influences on the television message has already been rationalised (chapters 2 and 3) in terms of intention and interpretation. Different levels of intention characterising a sign have been described (Jamieson, Thompson and Baggaley, 1976) in the following terms:

(1) Manifestation (no conscious or unconscious intention to signal). At the most primitive level all objects may be said to signal or signify their existence merely by their physical light-reflective properties. Unless one evokes an explanation for this based on paraphenomena, an observer would regard the light signals from objects as manifestations, not messages. The objects themselves would not be credited with an 'intention' to signal despite the fact that their existence becomes known to an observer, so in this case we can speak of 'nil intention'. The physical cues on television that viewers may take to be symbolic of a performer's credibility, for example, may convey no intentional message of this sort at all, though they may receive a completely meaningful interpretation.

(2) Broadcasting: (a) without a specific target audience. This second level of intention, which is really the beginning of a signalling system as commonly understood, occurs when cues and messages are generated consciously or unconsciously for a specific effect, but without a specific audience in mind. An example is the territorial warbling of birds. We can speak of this as broadcasting (casting broadly) with a specific if low-level intention. The term is thus used in its generic sense, and not in the limited sense of radio or television alone, although both senses are subsumed.

(3) Broadcasting: (b) with a specific target audience. This level still retains the property of broadcasting, but it bears the 'intention' of reaching a specific audience. It is goal-directed (cf. Mackay, 1972; and chapter 2), or, to put it another way, it is more finely focused. But as

153

distinct from the next, higher level of intention, it still lacks a co-operative device or 'feedback'. Conventional radio and television as a whole fall into this category and the more channels the broadcasting organisation controls, the more specific its output may become. Specificity here may be of a geographical nature (e.g. local radio) or may relate to material intended for particular age ranges or cultural groups. Even the merest of visual cues in the most fleeting of televised moments may carry a message with this level of intention.

(4) Two-way communication (containing interactive feedback). At this level we begin to expect co-operation between the sender and the receiver; it is the level at which 'feedback' is established and utilised, at which the receiver can check his interpretation of the message's meaning against the sender's intention, and at which we can say that conversation takes place.

In chapter 7 we discuss the current developments in technology that promise a rapid growth in interactive telecommunications systems over the next twenty years. Programme material broadcast over interactive channels in the future will belong not to the second and third levels of intention but to the level 4, and this critical change in the tele-communication milieu in which messages are conveyed will radically alter the predicted psychodynamic properties of the media.

The intentional characteristics of a sign or message thus defined express the factors underlying its transmission and the nature of the communi-cation channel established (chapter 2). Also determining its actual communication, on the other hand, are those many external/internal reception variables we have discussed in chapter 3. The 'noise' factors in communication (chapter 1) are the total range of unwanted variables affecting the interpretation and intention of a message alike − in the present terms they also are seen more explicitly in reference to both the source and the receiver of a message, rather than (according to the conventional model) as an abstract influence upon the intervening channel alone. But in order to elevate our set of terms regarding the dynamics of communication to a level at which they may be usefully manipulated in applied contexts henceforward, we must make one further theoretical connection. For lacking in the discussion hitherto has been a measuring device for the separate sciences of semiology and human processes (each with their attendant advantages and shortcomings) to make use of equally. How may we identify this? How have other thinkers approached the problem? Brémond (1966), objecting to the linearity and determinism of message analysis as we have done earlier in the book, argues the need to introduce *possibility* into the analysis, so that at each junction point in the message a finite range of alternative possibilities for its development is seen to be available. The prime thinker in these terms has been the social anthropologist Lévi-Strauss. To him, any observable phenomenon may be interpreted in a finite number of alternative ways; the interpretation chosen, and *ipso facto* the significance attributed to the observation, is the most probable one in this range of alternatives (Lévi-Strauss, 1969). The interpretation of significance in a communicated message may thus be defined (Leach, 1974) 'as a kind of algebraic matrix of possible permutations and combinations located in the unconscious "human mind"; the empirical evidence is merely an example of what is possible.'

A fundamental base for studies of the dynamic effects of television may thus be sought via the assessment of the intentions and interpretation of its messages in terms of probabilities. The implicit use of a language of probability by the semiologists has been indicated already, though skills in manipulating this language have been the more exclusive asset of scientific analysts rather than of the artist. Probability theory, however, provides a common language between them both with respect to semiological processes generally, and for our analyses of communication and the media in future contexts. The correct interpretation of a man as an expert on the basis of certain visual cues, for example, is regarded as being governed by the probability of an association between expertise and these signs in the natural world, and of the human error factors underlying their perception. (Similarly, the perception of a man as more credible because he is seen at a certain angle relates to the probability that this angle is constantly applied in presenting such men, e.g. in interview situations, over time.) At the one extreme of intention (level 1 above) where a sign is characterised by 'nil intention', being merely a 'manifestation', the measurement task is relatively simple, for the probability of the sign's occurrence may be estimated in terms of natural proportions alone. In this context, the probability of a particular interpretation of the sign may be estimated with recourse to the classical paradigms of experimental psychology (e.g. information theory: Cherry, 1957; Attneave, 1959; and signal detection theory: Swets, 1964). At the higher levels of intention, however, whereby signs are in various degrees actually communicated, the analysis becomes a more complicated question of the interplay between intention and interpretation jointly: but a quantifiable science of semiology may confidently attempt to identify the joint probabilities underlying communicated signs nonetheless. When the source of a sign is human, of course, the notion of its underlying intention may be grasped intuitively; though, as we have seen in chapter 2, the identification of the precise source of a message may, in broadcast communication contexts at least, be problematic. So in practice it is likely that semiological analyses of the media and their messages will concentrate on the psychodynamic interpretation processes specifically, rather than on the attempt to define intentions, characteristic of earlier determinist approaches. By the psychodynamic approach, analysts may conveniently choose to concentrate on the conventional codes used in communication (signs bearing a high probability of meaning in a given context); and they may examine the probability of particular interpretations of a code under specified conditions. For control over communication consists of maximising (by training procedures, for instance) the probability that the intentions conveyed by a given code are interpreted correctly, and it is from study of the contexts in which codes are maximally successful that the ability to predict and control communication effects will derive.

In the specific analysis of the dynamics of television, therefore, 'probabilistic semiology' is offered as a promising tool for future use. We speak of the television message as a collection of signs — some deliberately coded, others suggestive of meaning nonetheless — on which a particular interpretation is imposed; and on this basis we may develop the analysis of communication codes anticipated by Baggaley (1973b) and Hood (1975) — cf. chapter 3. The descriptive language of semiology à la Pierce (1940) provides a useful inroad to the problem, though it is suspected that the classical simplicity of de Saussure's terminology (1915) will yield itself most appropriately to quantification. The profound insights into human thought offered by Lévi-Strauss (1966) add a new dimension to our analysis of communication processes in the media context as in general: for Lévi-Strauss (1970) sees man's interpretation of the world not so much as a rational hypothetical process, as in personal construct theory, but as based on a collection of myths:

> I claim to show, not how men think in myths but how myths operate in men's minds without their being aware of the fact.

Certainly the experimental effects reported in chapter 4 may be interpreted more in terms of collective myth than in more rational terms. The assessment of a performer seen in profile as more expert and reliable because 'all experts are seen in profile' has been interpreted as being based upon an unconscious assessment of the probabilities of his characteristics in specific spatial and conventional contexts, and all of our empirical effects have similarly been explained in terms of context. The analysis of the effects of television will aim to identify the range of myths operating on the viewing experience and the dynamic changes that occur within them. Having glimpsed the dynamics of the viewing process by, for

156

example, a semiological approach, we may then begin to shape and control the effects of television themselves.

It is particularly intriguing at this time to note that the one school of thought — the French semiological tradition — had generated possibilities not only for the understanding of the communication processes in general, and for the analysis of mediated processes in particular, but also for the subsequent identification and control of media properties in specific styles of use henceforth. It is appropriate to end this chapter in this light, with a further reference to television's use in education, not only as an expedient tool but also as an object of study itself: the latter generates more effective control over the former, and the two avenues of study feed one another. The importance of the semiological approach for educational television is strongly indicated, as we write, by Jacquinot (1976, translation from the French):

> There is a lack of research into the exploitation of the specific properties of the medium in which meaning is embedded when it serves an instructional aim . . . Film has a capacity to achieve its instructional aims through the way the medium itself carries the meaning . . . [in educational television] one should find a style of production which does justice to the specific nature of the meaningfulness of the medium. It will then remain to put this hypothesis, which is theoretically based, to proof by experiment. (p.2/3)

By examining the properties of television in future contexts in the manner semiological theory suggests, we may surely approach a fuller realisation of its potential, and in the final chapter we therefore reappraise our position, examine current developments in communications technology, and consider the ethical issues that our work raises in the context of future broadcasting policy.

Summary

(1) In view of the medium's subtle psychological side-effects, the campaigning use of 'access television' requires close supervision and guidance. Due warning should be given to the users of access facilities of the effects that a lack of control over media presentation may have.

(2) Greater attention must be paid to the design of presentation techniques for television's use in education specifically if its value is to be guaranteed. Basic instructional functions must be identified which

television can effectively simulate in the over-burdened educational system of the future.

(3)   The pure and applied discipline of Communication Studies will provide a clearer understanding of media properties, and lead to a surer control of their effects in general. The processes and skills of mediation may be identified via simulation procedures.

(4)   A theoretical framework for the study of media effects is available in semiology, the study of signs and symbols. The range of terms on which traditional semiology is based, however, prevents its application in the study of human communication processes without certain modifications.

(5)   The dynamics of television may be described, predicted, monitored and controlled by a semiological approach quantified in terms of probability. In the study of communication dynamics generally, personal construct theory may be extended to take account of 'personal myths', as in social anthropology.

References

Attneave, F. (1959), *Applications of Information Theory to Psychology*, New York, Holt Rinehart.

Baggaley, J. P. (1972), report for the National Educational CCTV Association Research Group.

Baggaley, J. P. (1973a), 'Analysing TV presentation techniques for educational effectiveness', *Educational Broadcasting International*, vol. 8, no. 3.

Baggaley, J. P. (1973b), 'Developing an effective educational medium', *Programmed Learning and Educational Technology*, vol. 10.

Baggaley, J. P. (1975), 'Access to the looking glass', *Educational Broadcasting International*, vol. 8, no. 2.

Baggaley, J. P. and Duck, S. W. (1975a), 'Communication effectiveness in the educational media: three experiments', in Baggaley, J. P., Jamieson, G. H. and Marchant, H. (eds), *Aspects of Educational Technology VIII*, Bath, Pitman Press.

Baggaley, J. P., Jamieson, G. H. and Marchant, H. (eds) (1975), *Aspects of Educational Technology VIII*, Bath, Pitman Press.

Brémond, C. (1966), 'La logique des possibles narratifs', *Communications*, no. 8.

Brenes, A. (1975), 'Video-tape feedback effects on interpersonal perception accuracy and self-awareness', unpublished MSc thesis, University of Birmingham.

Bruner, J. S. and Goodman, C. C. (1947), 'Value and need as organising factors in perception', *J. Abn. Soc. Psychol.*, vol. 42.

Brynmor Jones Committee Report (1965), 'Use of audio visual aids in higher scientific education', HMSO.

Carpenter, E. (1976), *Oh, What a Blow that Phantom Gave Me!*, St Albans, Herts., Paladin.

Cherry, C. (1957), *On Human Communication,* New York, Wiley.

Cherry, C. (1973), 'Communication: science, art or technology?', paper read to the International Conference on the Future of Communication Studies, Heathrow, London.

Collins, R. (1975), 'Television and the people: access, participation and assimilation', *Screen Education*, no. 14.

Creaser, H. (1976), Audio Visual Centre, University of York: personal communication.

Goldwyn, E. (1974), 'Access television', *Educational Broadcasting International*, vol. 7, no. 4.

Groombridge, B. (1972), *Television and the People,* Harmondsworth, Penguin.

Hjelmslev, L. (1963), *Prolegomena to a Theory of Language,* Madison, The University of Wisconsin Press.

Holt, R. R. (1964), 'Imagery: the return of the ostracized', *Amer. Psychologist*, vol. 19.

Hood. S. (1975), 'Visual literacy examined', in Luckham, B. (ed.), *Proceedings of the Sixth Symposium on Broadcasting Policy – 'Audio-Visual Literacy',* University of Manchester.

Hooper, R. (1975), 'Computers and sacred cows', in Baggaley, J. P., Jamieson, G. H. and Marchant, H. (eds), *Aspects of Educational Technology VIII*, Bath, Pitman Press.

Jacquinot, G. (1976), 'Structures spécifiques du message audio-visuel didactique', paper presented to the International Conference on Evaluation and Research in Educational Broadcasting, Open University.

Jaensch, E. R. (1930), *Eidetic Imagery*, London, Kegan Paul.

Jamieson, G. H., Thompson, J. O. and Baggaley, J. P. (1976), 'Intention and interpretation in the study of communication', *Journal of Educational Television*, vol. 2, no. 1.

Kay, H., Dodd, B. and Sime, M. (1968), *Teaching Machines and Programmed Instruction*, Harmondsworth, Penguin.

Kelly, E. L. (1934), 'An experimental attempt to produce artificial chromaesthesia by the technique of the conditioned response', *J. Exper. Psychol.*, vol. 17.

Leach, E. (1974), *Lévi-Strauss,* London, Fontana.

Lévi-Strauss, C. (1966), *The Savage Mind*, London, Weidenfeld and Nicolson.

Lévi-Strauss, C. (1969), *Totemism*, Harmondsworth, Penguin.

Lévi-Strauss, C. (1970), *The Raw and the Cooked*, London, Cape.

Leytham, G. (1970), 'An audio-visual aids and programmed learning unit', *Medical and Biological Illustration*, vol. 20, no. 1.

Mackay, D. M. (1972), 'Formal analysis of communicative processes', in Hinde, R. A. (ed.), *Non-Verbal Communication*, Cambridge, Cambridge University Press.

Mackworth, J. F. (1970), *Vigilance and Attention*, Harmondsworth, Penguin.

Masterman, L. (1976), 'The educational simulation of TV news', *Journal of Educational Television*, vol. 2, no. 2.

Metz, C. (1974), *Film Language: A Semiotics of the Cinema*, New York, Oxford University Press.

Mohan, T. (1976), 'Media studies in vocationalism', *Journal of Educational Television*, vol. 2, no. 2.

Moss, J. R. (1972), 'Variables of CCTV presentation in higher education', report for the National Educational CCTV Association Research Group.

Pierce, C. S. (1955) (ed. J. Buchler), *Philosophical Writings of Pierce*, New York, Dover.

Propp, V. (1958), *Morphology of the Folktale*, Publication 10 of the Research Center in Anthropology, Folklore and Linguistics, Indiana University Press.

de Saussure, F. (1915), *Cours de Linguistique Générale*, Lausanne/Paris, Bally and Sechehaye.

Swets, J. A. (ed.) (1964), *Signal Detection and Recognition by Human Observers*, New York, Wiley.

Webster, B. R. and Cox, S. M. (1973), 'The value of colour in educational television', NCET Research Project Report.

Wollen, P. (1974), *Signs and Meaning in the Cinema*, London, Secker and Warburg.

Zeckhauser, S. H. (1972), 'A look at the media in higher education', *Programmed Learning and Educational Technology*, vol. 9.

7 Two-way mirror

Medium and message

Our aim in this book has been to indicate the dynamic subtleties of television's impact and the numerous psychological dimensions underlying it which previous research has overlooked. Our criticism of the traditional determinist approaches to media influence is that they leave out its most important determinant: the viewer. In social and perceptual psychology the individual's role in construing and adapting to his environment is now sufficiently well-established for his regular and normal psychological processes to be examined with respect to their likely role in the TV viewing process. In considering these processes we have suggested that the central element of the viewing experience (as of human behaviour in general) is the viewer's proclivity towards structure and hypothesis, his search for meaning. Small wonder, from this point of view, that viewers respond to the cues inherent in TV and use these cues to structure their reception of the more obvious message. Essentially, therefore, our analysis has centred on the dynamic effects of the imagery of television rather than its actual thematic message — and in this we do not simply say that the medium *is* the message: we say that the medium contributes to and structures the message by means of the imagery that it produces. Accordingly we wish to encourage new focal points in the analysis not only of television's overt thematic content, but also of the techniques used more covertly to present it, and the viewer's interpretation of the whole. We wish also to re-emphasise (cf. chapter 2) that the medium is not *ipso facto* the 'channel' of a particular message: the latter we regard as relating more broadly to the gulf between two communication agents that the medium is employed to bridge. As the sum of its mediating techniques the medium serves their intentions to communicate to the limit of its users' skills. Although the terms 'medium', 'message' and 'channel' have been popularly confused in the past, there are crucial distinctions between them which should henceforward be observed.

If forced to define the actual determinants of the TV message, we would thus credit the medium with a vital though partial role in its impact only: for any technology may exert different effects on its viewers according to the socio-psychological processes underpinning their perception of it. We attribute the inconclusiveness and low esteem of much media research in the past (chapter 1) to the fact that the conventional analyses of media subject matter alone are an inadequate basis for studies of media effects. Once based on a knowledge of the processes by which TV content is interpreted, however, we feel that analysis of its impact will become immediately more viable, and that the practical value of media research will be strengthened. The advantage of a multi-disciplinary approach to the study of the dynamics of television lies in the fact that attention to the internal processes of the viewer can be co-equal with that given to the most specific questions of media production: now that the technology is available by which to examine the effects of media imagery itself, they must be studied in their natural interaction with content effect if communication research is fundamentally to affect the policies and strategies of media usage to come. This is especially the case in view of the fact that the impact of modern media is (for reasons discussed in chapter 5) so immense both at the individual and global societal levels.

Yet in the process of studying the effects of television at any level certain problems arise. One recurrent theme of this book has been the impossibility of ever drawing completely clear lines between the various types of TV content since its elements are continually subject to combination and re-combination, and often cannot even be defined in isolation. The attempt to impose even the broadest of labels on the elements of a dynamic process may be equally hopeless: witness the indistinction of persuasive and non-persuasive broadcasting in the context of 'informative' programmes. In an important, if philosophical, sense *any* informative medium is also a persuasive medium since information (or, more accurately, *new* information) can impinge upon a person's psychological processes only by inducing some change in them. In other words, before an individual can assimilate some new information or before he can be affected by it, he too must undergo dynamic change. Of course, even when no conscious effort to change the individual is being made, changes that may elude description are permanently occurring with the simple passage of time. In the strict sense that it is impossible for a man to step into the same river twice man and his environment are never the same for two consecutive instants. Consequently, when an individual receives (and, moreover, is persuaded to assimilate) new information, his psychological constitution is essentially altered; but while the elements and structure of a dynamic process are momentarily elusive, the types of change it effects may actually demonstrate a common logic.

In the particular context of television, for example, there is a more important and less abstruse sense in which all communications are persuasive as well as informative. As we have argued earlier, the message of a TV programme (or an advert, or a book, or a piece of advice from a friend) can be both specific ('X has died'; 'Buy Blanco'; 'I recommend you not to apply for *that* job') and general ('All news is bad'; 'Replace products at yearly intervals even if they are not worn out'; 'Wealth corrupts'). Both types of message elicit correspondingly different types of effects simultaneously. Particularly in the case of TV, it is important to know that attitudes about general issues, which admit greater argument, can be influenced by the way in which TV *presents* the information (see chapters 4 and 5): such effects may seem marginal but, in fact, they are probably the most insidious effects that the medium exerts, since they mature only gradually, influencing viewers' attitudes as the effects of presentation conventions are gradually absorbed. They are long term 'sleeper effects' (chapter 5), and as such are difficult even to recognise, let alone measure.

This observation highlights a weakness or omission in the traditional analysis of communication. From chapter 2, Lasswell's (1948) famous dictum — that communication is a matter of who says what in which channel to whom and with what effect — will be recalled. Our research and analysis indicate at least two omissions here. For one thing it is unfortunate that Lasswell concentrates on the *declared content* of the message rather than on the performance associated with it. (He does not even ask 'who says what and *how*?'.) We would suggest that the performer's characteristics and the mode of his presentation to the audience are fundamentally relevant to the message's reception, and cannot simply be subsumed under some general rubric that concerns itself with *what* he says *in what channel.* On this count Lasswell's work could be extended to read 'Who says what, how, *in what context* and channel, to whom and with what effect?'. But even this solution is clearly less than complete in the light of the work we have reported and the copious psychological literature that suggested it. Our major emphasis, falling upon the viewer and his processes of anticipation, hypothesis and structure, indicates a powerful elemental force in the impact of the message that Lasswell's analysis passes over almost lightly. But to argue that analysis of the audience is covered by 'to whom' is to confound the sociological and psychological bases of television's impact entirely, encouraging a simple blanket definition of the type, role, status, occupation, etc. of the audience members rather than study of their psychological needs and processing powers. Since the number of unknowns the latter involves is somewhat too extensive to be left to the tail end of the empirical question, we would suggest that the order of priorities in media research be reversed, and the viewer's psychodynamic role in TV's impact explicitly acknowledged in the study of '*who* infers *what* from *what presentation* in *what context* and *channel* and having *what needs*?'. When the media's impact is queried in this way the rider 'with what effect' is redundant; more precise effects than the question envisages may not be manifested until long after their origin when it is far too late to connect them with it anyway.

Whilst the point we make concerning communication studies may seem rather pessimistic, the above approach does suggest specific ways in which their scope and value may be examined. For example, it emphasises that specific attention to viewers' motivational states at particular times, being related to their general disposition to structure and hypothesise, may give pointers to the effective development of certain types of educational TV material. Anxiety in an enforced viewing situation will clearly increase (a) with the complexity of the topic under discussion; (b) with the importance of the topic to the individual viewer; (c) according to other factors known to affect the need for structure generally (Johnson, 1976); and (d) according to factors affecting the need for comparison with other people (Festinger, 1954). These are the factors determining the viewer's reliance on the cues TV offers him; and it is to these extra dimensions of television's dynamism that research attention must now be turned so that producers may harness the cues in developing the medium's influence generally. In deciding whether such manipulation is good or bad, we would line ourselves up behind Qualter (1968), stressing that the morality of a particular influence stems *in part* from the intentions behind it. We have continually emphasised that at present the techniques we have studied do appear to be used innocently; and in educational contexts the use of standard techniques to improve the viewers' trust in material as well as its visual interest would be an added bonus. However, media practitioners may easily transgress into less ethical uses of presentation techniques when decisions become difficult concerning the thin line between education and information on the one hand, and propagandist influence on the other. It is our belief that intentional manipulation of a TV presenter's image (by means of the cues that we have examined, and others equally effective that remain to be discovered) can have both negative and positive effects — and the degree of intention behind the use of such cues helps to draw the line that arbiters of TV ethics require.

Ethics of media control

Any study which aims to improve the ways in which a communication

164

medium may be used must face up to the ethical questions of media control and the possibility that particularly effective presentation techniques may be abused. The obviously disturbing implication of our work is that presentation strategies affect the TV viewer subliminally. This was brought home most forcibly by the results of the multifactorial experiment (chapter 4) which showed that the viewers perceived one style of appeal as more favourable, yet still responded most generously to a different style. The experiment also showed that such effects are surprisingly resilient in combination: though they might well have reversed or cancelled one another out when applied in a different context using a different performer or text, they withstood the test (on this occasion at least) and with very little further effort might well prove capable of fortifying one another. In the advertising context the effects of subliminal presentation techniques — now illegal — have been studied at length. Of course, there is a logical difference between the type of presentation effect we have studied above, and those which require legislation, for the one is produced by strategies regarded as quite innocent in their effect (upon visual interest), while the other is based on more calculated rationales for the actual change of attitudes. And as long as the prime criterion for the use of particular TV techniques is that of visual interest alone its further subliminal effects are unlikely to justify actual moral concern. Besides, as we have seen throughout, the viewer will draw a range of the most inventive inferences from any detail or juxtaposition of details one may care to give him. Hence our observation in chapter 4 that 'all television is subliminal advertising' even when it is not consciously intended as such (cf. Potter, 1975), by dint of this tremendous visual suggestibility on the viewer's part: our experiments in chapter 4 have borne out this point. Thus attempts to curtail the possible distorting effects of TV imagery by its scrupulous control would be at once.futile and potentially distorting themselves.

The ethical laws of media control are obviously as incapable of general definition as the practical rules of media effect: both logically depend on the context and purpose of the material presented, and must be drawn up according to the pragmatic philosophy we prescribed for the study of the dynamics of television in chapter 6. The same applies to the ethics of media research: by warning of television's subtle propensities to distort and coerce, research may certainly be the means by which abuses are first suggested but it may also uncover guidelines for the medium's beneficial use, and should be judged in this light. The negative potential of media strategies may be countered by the expedient of instructing the audience as to the possible effects. However dangerous the negative side of media research and development may be, both should clearly continue on the basis that the public needs and 'has the right to know' of any potential effects against which it should be forearmed. Influences of the type we have studied may therefore be rendered less susceptible to abuse through conscious and active efforts by broadcasting authorities to inform the viewing public about them. An increase in media literacy and 'training' of the viewer and the producer is called for in this context as in that of TV's educational influence discussed earlier.

The need for active attention to the problems of 'media literacy' is particularly vital in view of the political and propagandist uses to which the medium can be put. Whilst our suggestions in relation to other areas of broadcasting are relatively mild, we feel strongly that deliberate and manipulative use of their techniques in political connections needs to be more carefully scrutinised. Whilst it is not appropriate for researchers on TV to dictate particular styles of TV debate, it is still necessary for them to point out the consequences of technical strategies such as those we have examined. The implications of our results for political broadcasting, as in the context of appeals for cash, include the fact that the most successful subversive techniques cause viewers to pay attention to the 'wrong' parts of the TV broadcast when assessing it: being uninformed in media practice they fail to be aware of the parts which are actually influencing their behaviour. We would not overestimate the results of this tendency but, taking heed of the fact that elections are decided by those who do change their mind, that people who change their minds are often even then uncommitted, that indecision evokes the perpetual search for structure, and that structure is provided by the techniques we have examined, we feel that the likely implications of presentation technique are an essential issue for future broadcasting policymakers to consider in more detail. Since counter-legislation in itself involves political decisions that may prove discriminating, we feel that the proposal for more vigorous attempts to be made to increase viewers' media awareness is the only solution to the problem. We suggest the indisputable wisdom of periodic research reports on the ways that the techniques of media such as television are developing: a permanent introspectiveness by the media and their research organisations with regard to media dynamics in general. The form of such reports may vary from the documentary styles of programmes already popular (*Inside the News, Film as Evidence,* etc. cf. chapter 1) to brief cameo inserts between programmes informing viewers about the medium itself as well as its forthcoming attractions. Broadcasters themselves might certainly be reluctant to give away the secrets of their technique in certain contexts: as we have seen, the media's artistic use actually relies on the preservation of a certain technical mystique. But in their role as informers of society (as opposed to entertainers) it is completely within their own interests to examine the influence of their techniques and priorities in informative contexts at least, and to extend public knowledge of them.

As a further step in the interests of media development we urge a consideration both by official bodies, broadcasting policymakers, researchers and viewers themselves of the broader assumptions underlying the stylistics of broadcast material at an even broader level: not only with respect to the specific presentation techniques we have emphasised experimentally, but also in terms of the equity and constraints of programming as a whole. Is the customary subservience of TV news programming to a rigid time-base, for example, completely necessary? It is certainly not a desirable feature of current practice in which the informative, entertainment and (in some organisations) commercial functions of television are awkwardly compromised: the length of time usually given to news coverage – a fixed time, it should be noted, which rarely varies with the amount of material available to fill it – is determined solely by the balance between informative and entertainment broadcasting decided by the schedule controllers on political criteria. The need for such decisions is invidious. If we had the option, would we ethically choose to present the news within the same schedule as the entertainment forms of television at all? When major news breaks the main bulletins are certainly capable of extension and special 'newsflashes' are presented: but care is taken that programmes are only interrupted at points where a break was scheduled anyway – and the very juxtaposition of world events and a barrage of commercial and entertainment content invariably trivialises. As has become clear, news productions are gradually coming more and more to be dressed in the technical frills and furbelows of their entertainment cousins: an obvious product of their conjunction within the same political framework. The danger that entertainment and commercial criteria in TV policy will eventually dominate, as in American networks (R. Williams, 1974), already seems to be materialising.

We may cite a recent example of this in British television. The splashdown of the Apollo astronauts after their rendezvous with the Russian Soyuz craft in 1975 was elaborately anticipated by the TV news departments and the customary programme schedule upended in the process. *News at Ten* on the independent networks prepared for the event with scale models, animations, pundits, satellite link-up for live coverage, and a sizeable extension of its time allocation – it then missed the actual splashdown because it occurred fifty seconds too early during the

167

commercial break. (Instant replay was naturally available, but this would surely have been a sufficient method of coverage for the event anyway.) Even once the deliberate decision to accord the event special treatment had been made, the basic conflict between TV's informative and commercial functions on the one networked time-base overrode it, as the tyrants time and the sponsors imposed the ultimate presentation constraints. Evidently the commercials cannot wait for the news as easily as the news can wait for the interval in *Coronation Street*. We are forced to the conclusion that within the same schedule TV presentations serving distinctly separate informative and entertainment functions in this way are basically incompatible. When they are compromised their priorities must be rated on some artificial basis of equivalence: and any means of countering the biasing influences on media presentation that arise in consequence must certainly be examined in future broadcasting contexts.

Transparency regained

The political system in Utopia is one which fulfils all individual and social needs, yet experiences no internal conflict and is self-preserving. The broadcasting system of the future which best approaches this ideal will be one in which the media's main functions are fulfilled without any demand for compromise, each using a technology that can evolve and be applied according to its own criteria. Accordingly, the entertainment and informative functions of media must be capable of separation in practice. In chapter 2 we saw that the functions of the television message can be distinguished and separately examined quite readily; confusion between the thematic components of TV content having a particular function may occur, yet as long as the critical factor of presentation technique is taken into account, confusions of function itself do not. Definitions of programme theme in isolation, as per traditional content analyses, are clearly inadequate: not only the theme but also its function and the techniques used in conveying it must be identified if its effects on the viewer are ever to be fully understood. (The study of TV's dynamics in this way is also sure to lead to improvements in the predictive value of audience research methodology: cf. chapters 2 and 6.) Of course, the viewing audience itself is a more difficult animal to analyse: it is amorphous, uncommitted in its tastes, unreliable in its responses and involved in the viewing experience at many different levels. The efficiency of broadcast material can only be defined if the extent to which it caters for particular audience needs can be measured. As Worcester (1976)

168

indicates, the failure to define minority elements within the audience prevents researchers from realising this objective at present. Once the dynamics of television and its viewing experience are analysed and can be predicted, however, the technologies of television can be applied in catering for the audience's needs ever more efficiently.

In fact the facilities are already available for a totally novel form of telecommunication, tailor-made for the needs of the individual in society as well as 'the mass'. In the early 1970s, major developments have taken place in the resources enabling storage and ready accessibility of information (Whitaker, 1973). One multi-lens scanning device permits 600 pages of information to be read from a single sheet; another device stores 1,000 colour images in an audio cassette. On the general market, video cassette and disc facilities are available at surprisingly low costs: laser-red discs, for example, give approximately forty-five minutes' playing time at a cost of a few pence. New video-printing facilities allow the transfer of one tape to others (e.g. ten at once) by their simple passage through the same magnetic or thermal field. For video recording there are fully portable colour television cameras, cameras that can see in the dark, and broadcast quality machines that once cost twice as much as they do now. Public television screens twenty-four feet in width have been developed, as though mindful of the conditions once predicted for 1984. All are facilities with obvious applications in both domestic and educational use — though even these, as mere extensions of existing communications technology, may soon be outmoded.

For some of the most fascinating developments of all allow any display (auditory and/or visual) to be broken down into digital information for storage and subsequent reconstitution in a different form. Such technology has boundless possibilities. Old and deteriorating recordings may be encoded at microwave band width and reconstituted free from interference. An audio tape recorder is available with a digital store capable of speeding up and slowing down music, for instance, *without* altering its pitch. Most amazingly, it will be possible to convert the contents of, for example, videotape on to paper punch tape, which may be sent through the post, re-synthesised, and played back on video machinery with which the original equipment is totally incompatible. The most important consequence of such innovation is the freedom it provides from the traditional constraints of TV scheduling. Television material may be played and replayed in the viewer's own time. Even styles of instantaneous news transmission may be envisaged free of the distortions that arise when news is constrained by a fixed time and duration as at present (cf. above). Ceefax and Oracle, two rival services for data and facsimile transmission already made available by the two British broadcasting organisations, provide the television viewer with news, weather and traffic reports, sports results, programme schedules, and many other types of information on request (cf. Brown, 1975). If such facilities, at present purely alpha-numeric, were extended to include film and aural materials as well, there would be little need for the traditional form of news presentation at all. For there is logically no limit to the types and extent of the services that ultimately may be requested via television in this way. Shopping orders may be placed, bank statements requested, medical and other opinions consulted, aural and visual material selected for all purposes. For televisual technology is already fully two-way, allowing the public the vital outlet to check and thereby control the information it receives. Only the expense of the appropriate instruments prevents every home from enjoying standard videophone and teletype facilities whereby the world is its oyster. The combined potential of digital and cable techniques may eventually render even satellite communication outmoded (cf. Exwood, 1974). By the year 2000 it is estimated that, for £10 per head of the population, multi-purpose communication devices might link every building in the land. The viewer of television really bent on access to the medium (cf. chapter 6) could then prepare and transmit his own TV programmes anywhere at will!

Of course, such uses of the new technology are all pure pipedreams and will remain so for many good reasons. As with all innovations, the existence of particular facilities is of no avail unless the skills for their use are developed also. Moreover, the total accessibility of material and the freedom to use it whenever desired often renders its use less appealing. The citizens of Pisa, for whom the Leaning Tower is permanently accessible, have far less desire to climb it than the tourist, forced by time and his schedule to do so while he may. We feel therefore that the faith vested in the potential of new access systems in education will prove over-optimistic. In educational institutions throughout the United States (Hooper, 1969), sophisticated television installations lie embarrassingly idle: teachers are not compelled to use televisual aids as it was assumed they would, for they have discovered that TV production is a skilled and complex business, and that it takes hundreds more man-hours to design and execute an effective TV programme than it does to address a class in the traditional manner.

Moreover, the advent of new systems invariably meets opposition. Even a relatively simple modern development, the video cassette recorder, had been branded illegal by copyright regulations in some of the very contexts where it can prove most valuable. Each of the broadcasting organisations declares its intention to educate via a wide variety of different types of programme, but only the most rigidly defined programmes (for schools, the Open University, etc.) can be recorded for use in the classroom, and then at a price. As we have seen throughout the present book, the only just criteria for a programme's educational value is the intention underlying its use. Even the distinction between educational and propagandist material is moot, as was indicated in chapter 5, and urgent attention to current copyright legislation is now required. In the United States a certain relaxation of copyright provisions is becoming evident as we write — the NBC for example, has begun to grant licences to educational and other institutions to videotape a broad range of news and current affairs programmes off-air for non-profit purposes. It is to be hoped that the British broadcasting organisations will follow suit, so that the full value of the new technical developments can be realised without delay.

Of course the pessimist's view of media development will be that however promising new resources may seem to be, their powers will inevitably be exploited in the user's interest rather than the consumer's. R. Williams (1974) indicates the extent to which media effects may be steered against the public interest at both local and national levels. The answer, as before, is obviously to educate and arm society in advance against the effects it might experience, and it is the broadcasters' clear responsibility to undertake whatever measures prove necessary in this respect, rendering their own intentions and the needs of society ever clearer. Certainly the gradual devolution of the broadcast networks since the 1960s has created possibilities for more effective community participation in the media than existed previously — though, as we indicated in chapter 6, the provision of uncontrolled access to television may suffer critical repercussions. The most effective uses of television in the community at present are achieved when the ultimate responsibility for programme planning and production is retained by the networks. The Dutch community action programme *Werwinkel* is a prime example of a successful project of this type: in effect it presents the viewers with their own reflected image, helps to identify their needs and assists in organising the appropriate action. Granada-TV's *Reports Action* series, and similar ventures in other IBA regions, have followed this lead, marshalling hospital visitors, heavy labour for refuse tip clearance, help with playgroups, etc., with immense success. Such examples present the more optimistic face of media development through which the media professionals and their audience may ultimately come to full understanding. As technological possibilities are gradually assimilated, and the techniques for their use defined, the dynamic powers and effects of a medium such as television will continually be reshaped. But as long as the intentions of the media producers remain evident to their audience, and the latter's fluctuating needs are permanently clear to the broadcasters, the medium will convey a clear message, free from dynamic 'noise', effectively transparent.

In the informative function of television at least, transparency must eventually be the medium's essence. The need for greater communication between the users and their audience in this way is sometimes apparent in TV's artistic development also. It is all very well for a medium to achieve artistic status as defined by its users and the intentions they bring to it but if the audience cannot understand the art, in its own terms at least, then the medium is failing. It is unfortunate that much of the coding of televised material at present seems deliberately designed to encourage a quite passive reaction, for an art form can easily overstep the bounds of good faith which the audience places in it and become so opaque that its mysteries are impenetrable. And when the language of forms a medium uses becomes so opaque that the need for it to be explained is felt, then it has certainly reached the point where transparency must be regained. As we have attempted to indicate in this book, one of the most powerful sources of television's dynamics is the audience itself. The traditional determinist view of television in society — in which its *Weltanschauung* or world-view is regarded as causal to the social condition — thus presents one side of the problem only. And when we discuss the effects of television in society henceforward we must be careful not to apply a simple one-way determinism, but to question the viewer's contribution to the experience and the way in which he engages in and shapes the media art as participant in the producer—audience interaction. When the intentions of each can be interpreted by both and understanding is effectively two-way, then the medium of television will be transparent indeed. When the needs of each can accurately be predicted, its reflected images will be free from distortion. For entertainment purposes, the use of television techniques according to criteria of novelty and unpredictability will continue to be appropriate. But used for informative purposes they must be predictable to producer and audience alike, so that the dynamics of television may be contained. The techniques that harness the medium's dynamic properties to the full may ultimately provide better teaching

> In their majestic unaffected style,
> Than all the oratory of Greece and Rome.
> In them is plainest taught, and easiest learnt. (Milton)

Summary

(1) In general, the medium is a part-determinant of the message, structuring it via the imagery it produces. But if the dynamics of television are to be controlled, it is also necessary to study the viewer, his needs and their influence on the message's interpretation.

(2) The ethics of media control are dictated by the intentions underlying it, and the audience's sensitivity to media effects. Future attention to wide-ranging aspects of TV presentation is therefore urged.

(3) As communications technology develops, the dynamics of television will continue to fluctuate. They may be harnessed for the public good as long as the intentions of the producer and viewer are clear to both.

References

Brown, D. (1975), 'In the gap between the pictures — Teletext', *Video and Audio-Visual Review*, July.

Exwood, M. (1974), 'Cable television', *The Royal Television Society Journal,* vol. 15, no. 2.

Festinger, L. (1954), 'The theory of social comparison processes', *Human Relations*, vol. 7.

Hooper, R. (1969), 'A diagnosis of failure', *AV Communication Review*, vol. 17.

Johnson, F. N. (1976), 'Manic depression: a catastrophe model', *IRCS J. Med. Science*, vol. 4.

Lasswell, H. D. (1948), 'The structure and function of communications', in Bryson, L. (ed.), *The Communication of Ideas*, New York, Harper.

Potter, J. (1975), 'ITV: critics and viewers', *Independent Broadcasting*, 4.

Qualter, T. H. (1968), *Propaganda and Psychological Warfare*, New York, Random House.

Whitaker, P. (1973), 'A survey of technical innovations', paper to the Annual Conference of National Educational CCTV Association, University of Sussex.

Williams, R. (1974), *Television: Technology and Cultural Form*, London, Fontana.

Worcester, R. M. (1976), 'Where ratings don't rule', *The Observer*, 11 April.

Index

The authors

Jon Baggaley is lecturer in Communication Studies at the University of Liverpool and Editor of the *Journal of Educational Television*. He is currently Director of a Social Science Research Council project on the effects of television production techniques. His published work includes material on educational technology and the psychology of music.

Steve Duck is lecturer in Psychology at the University of Lancaster where he works on the effects of television and the study of friendship formation. His publications include two books and numerous articles on interpersonal attraction and personal construct theory.

Other SAXON HOUSE publications

Hodges, M.	*Multinational corporations and national governments*
Liggins, D.	*National economic planning in France*
Friedly, P. H.	*National policy responses to urban growth*
Madelin, H.	*Oil and politics*
Tilford, R. (ed.)	*The Ostpolitik and political change in Germany*
Friedrichs, J., H. Ludtke	*Participant observation*
Fitzmaurice, J.	*The party groups in the European parliament*
Brown, J., G. Howes (eds)	*The police and the community*
Lang, R. W.	*The politics of drugs*
Denton, F. T., B. G. Spencer	*Population and the economy*
Dickinson, J. P. (ed.)	*Portfolio analysis*
Wilson, D. J.	*Power and party bureaucracy in Britain*
Wabe, J. S.	*Problems in manpower forecasting*
Willis, K. G.	*Problems in migration analysis*
Farnsworth, R. A.	*Productivity and law*
Shepherd, R. J.	*Public opinion and European integration*
Richardson, H. W.	*Regional development policy and planning in Spain*
Sant, M. (ed.)	*Regional policy and planning for Europe*
Thorpe, D. (ed.)	*Research into retailing and distribution*
Dickinson, J. P.	*Risk and uncertainty in accounting and finance*
Hey, R. D., T. D. Davies (eds)	*Science, technology and environmental management*
Britton, D. K., B. Hill	*Size and efficiency in farming*
Buchholz, E., et al	*Socialist criminology*
Paterson, W. E.	*The SPD and European integration*
Blohm, H., K. Steinbuch (eds)	*Technological forecasting in practice*
Piepe, A., et al	*Television and the working class*
Goodhardt, G. J., et al	*The television audience*
May, T. C.	*Trade unions and pressure group politics*
Labini, P. S.	*Trade unions, inflation and productivity*
Casadio, G. P.	*Transatlantic trade*
Whitehead, C. M. E.	*The U.K. housing market*
Balfour, C.	*Unions and the law*